W9-BEG-353

EVERYTHING
YOU NEED TO KNOW ABOUT
COLLECTING

CHRISTMAS
COLLECTIBLES

THE TARON COLLECTION

EVERYTHING
YOU NEED TO KNOW ABOUT
COLLECTING

CHRISTMAS COLLECTIBLES

Copyright©1998 by Dr. James Beckett

All rights reserved under International
and Pan-American Copyright Conventions.

Published by:
Beckett Publications
15850 Dallas Parkway
Dallas, TX 75248

ISBN: 1-887432-57-4

Beckett® is a registered trademark of Beckett Publications.

*Everything You Need To Know About Collecting
Christmas Collectibles*

The prices on the following pages are based solely on the
knowledge and experience of the authors and dealers
across the country.
All figures are in U.S. dollars and are for entertaiment
and informational purposes only.

First Edition: October 1998
Printed in Canada

Beckett Corporate Sales and Information
(972) 991-6657

BECKETT

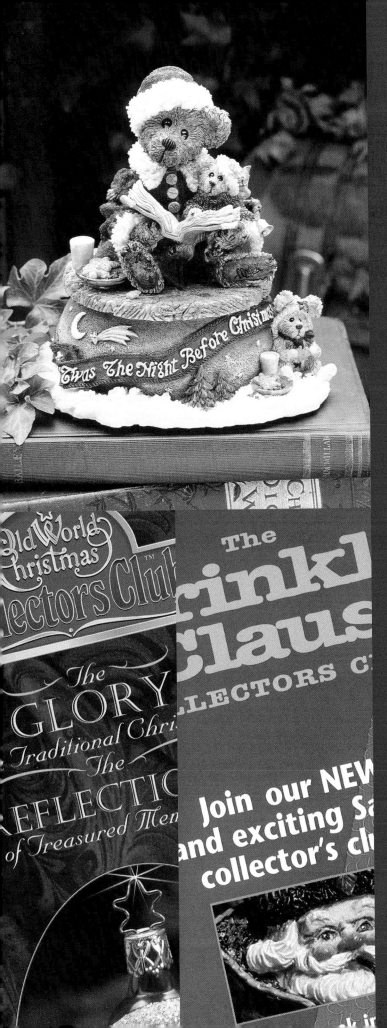

CONTENTS

Introduction: Christmas Collectibles

by Susan K. Elliott

s there any other word in the English language that is so richly colored with both memories and possibilities? We remember our own Christmases and the hundreds we've seen in movies and art, all colored by scenes of swirling snow falling on Christmas Eve and myriad other heartwarming images —presents under the decorated tree, the gathering of friends and family, quiet Christmas mornings filled with promise and hope.

Christmas appeals to collectors at all levels of the senses, and the special time of year allows us to relive memories as well as plan for future celebrations that comfort us with their familiarity.

Featured Collectibles

In this book you'll find a survey of the kaleidoscope of Christmas collectibles available today. The unprecedented growth in Christmas collecting in the last two and a half decades has inspired a talented generation of artists to reinterpret our Christmas dreams and desires in every imaginable medium. You can enjoy the traditional German Steinbach nutcrackers like the one immortalized by the classic Christmas ballet or the delicate, or admire the colorful blown glass of Christopher Radko ornaments made in Europe. You can take comfort from the innocence of figures from Cherished Teddies, I.M. Hummel and Possible Moments. You can smile at the whimsical figures from Charming Tails and

Boyd's Bears.

If you've always loved Christmas, this book will introduce you to companies and series you may have overlooked, or known just a little about. For example, in the last few years Patricia Breen ornaments from Poland have become so avidly collected that it's not unusual for collectors to order an entire blown-glass line sight unseen more than a year in advance. And if you love various lighted villages from Department 56, maybe you'd like to discover the Colonial Village of Geo. Z. Lefton and its 90 Christmas-themed buildings and 42 citizens and accessories.

You'll also be reunited with old friends such as Hallmark Keepsake Ornaments, which have captured collectors' hearts for 25 years now. With many ongoing conventions, swap and sell shows and active trading on the secondary market, Hallmark Keepsake Ornaments have ascended to the pinnacle of Christmas ornament collectibles status.

Two of the more valuable Keepsake ornaments capture the nostalgia of the holidays and also illustrate the enduring appeal of Hallmark and Christmas collectibles as a whole. The 1982 Tin Locomotive, first edition, originally sold for $13 and now sells for nearly $700. The 1977 Betsey Clark, fifth edition, was a $3.50 ornament that now commands a price of more than $400.

Those classic ornaments and others are discussed in the Hallmark section written by Meredith DeGood, nationally recognized Hallmark expert and co-owner of The Baggage Car antique collectibles shop. She is joined in the book by other Christmas-theme collectibles experts, who supply product overviews and selective pricing of the most popular items at retail and on the secondary market.

Please bear in mind that values are for items in Mint condition and that flaws and damage reduce the selling price of a piece. Also, values are full selling prices at time of publication, and lower prices can be found through

research firm. In 1996 alone, Christmas decorations totaled an astounding $4.3 billion in consumer sales, and items produced as collections or series for collecting accounted for $1.1 billion, up 21 percent over the previous year.

The manufacturers featured in this book comprise many of the more popular contemporary Christmas collectibles, but there are other lines being explored by collectors and attracting new hobbyists each month.

Christmas plates, after all, were the start of the collecting industry we know today. In 1895, the Danish porcelain maker Bing & Grondahl capitalized on the custom of the wealthy to give food on special plates to servants each Christmas. Bing & Grondahl offered the first dated Christmas plate, Beyond the Frozen Window, for a modest 50 cents. If you could find one of those 2,000 early editions, it would be worth about $5,000. This dated blue-and-white plate series continues today, making it the oldest series in production

To thousands of people around the world, the blue-and-white of these traditional designs (along with the "newer" series begun by Royal Copenhagen in 1908) mean Christmas.

extensive shopping.

Melanie Benham covers the shimmering array of blown-glass ornaments such as Radko and Polonaise from Kurt Adler. Melanie and her husband write the newsleter Glitter, and are the largest secondary market brokers for contemporary blown-glass ornaments in the United States. Other nationally recognized contributors are Dean Genth of Miller's Hallmark and Gift Gallery, who covers the diverse lines of figurines; Susan Ford Wiese, the author of Nutcracker News, a newsletter on her specialty; and

Matthew Rothman of the Lighthouse Trading Company, who discusses and prices architecture ranging from Department 56 buildings to lighthouses from Harbour Lights.

Other Options

It must be pointed out that all contemporary Christmas collectibles are not featured in this book. Such an undertaking would require a book from two to three times the size of this one. For Christmas is the No. 1 collecting category in the country, as reported by Unity Marketing, a market

Families can trace the years of their lives through the dated Christmas plates that were hung one each year. Collectors quickly distinguish one series from another because the RC designs feature an evergreen border with a star at the top, while art on the B&G plates includes the words "Jule Aften" and the year at the bottom. Subjects range from Danish holiday scenes to angels and woodland creatures. Back issues can often be found in antique stores as well as collectibles shops.

These classic plates have been joined by hundreds of plates series from companies around the world. Today collectors can find beautiful angels, Santas, children at Christmas, nostalgic snow-covered cottages and any other yule subject one could desire.

Because collectors enjoy collectibles in multiple mediums, favorite artists such as Thomas Kinkade offer Christmas subjects in more than one collectible version, including plates, graphics, ornaments and lighted houses. This certainly broadens the decorating possiblities.

Other popular artists such as Terry Redlin, James Christensen and Charles Wysocki are delighting collectors with their annual Christmas prints, capturing images of greater complexity in this larger-size format.

For figurine collectors, The Greenwich Workshop Collection has begun to attract dedicated collectors in recent years with high-quality porcelains by some of its most popular graphics artists, including James Christensen, Scott Gustafson, and Will

Bullas. Figurine collectors have also catapulted the Seraphim Angel collection from Roman to superstar status, along with Dean Griff's Charming Tails for Fitz & Floyd.

Many collectors specialize in nativities alone, and numerous makers have added to that specialty with their own distinctive renditions. Fontanini has become especially popular in recent years with its offerings of various sizes in popularly priced resin. (Look closely in the first "Home Alone" movie and you'll see a life-size Fontanini nativity.)

Then there are those collectors who enjoy the simple grace of ornaments, such as Swarovski Silver Crystal, produced in beautiful Wattens, Austria, which is near Innsbruck. The secondary market for Swarovski has been growing, as evidenced by the strong secondary market prices for the older annual Christmas ornaments. The Christmas ornaments initially were not received with overwhelming enthusiasm, but people have began to rethink adding the annual ornaments to their collection.

One of the determining factors that aroused interest was the addition of the logo to the ornaments in addition to the annual date. The 1989 Annual

Swarovski Ornament sells for $350. The 1981 Annual Ornament also sells for $350, making these two items the best secondary market Swarovski Christmas issues.

Whatever the focus of your interests, you may collect purely for your own enjoyment or with definite thoughts of investment potential. Either way, it's rewarding to find out that a Hallmark treetopper you bought a few years ago for $9 is now worth more than $300, or that your Margaret Furlong annual bisque angel ornament collection is highly valued by other collectors. And who wouldn't like to discover that the lighted church that's been the centerpiece of their Christmas mantle display since 1992 is a St. Mark's Cathedral from the Department 56 Christmas in the City collection, now worth more than $1,400?

The world of clubs offers specialized groups focused specifically on Christmas as well as Christmas combined with other subjects. The number of clubs available has exploded in recent years, with many special items available only to club members, such as the charter year Angels We Have Heard on High ornament from Christopher Radko that now brings $350-$500 (up from an issue price of $50). For more information on clubs, please see the special section in the back of the book. It's interesting to note that of all the collector clubs available, a Christmas club — the Hallmark Keepsake Ornament Collector's Club — is now the largest of all with more than 250,000 members.

How to Collect

Because so many of us have begun Christmas collections without any thought of eventual monetary value, we may be only vaguely aware of the worth of pieces we've accumulated over the years. This book will guide you in determing values for some of the variety of Christmas collectibles that you may own.

For additional values, refer to current price guides in your local bookstore, collectibles magazines or newsletters that specialize in individual lines, collector clubs, software programs that include price guides, or on-line sources such as chat rooms or collector forums.

If you do decide to sell some of your collection or purchases additions, you can turn to a variety of sources, including classified ads in collector publications, national collector exchanges, swap and sell events at major collectible shows, Internet postings, club publications or retailers. Keep in mind that you'll get the highest price from another collector, since a retailer or exchange will have to offset the price of doing business.

There is obviously no guarantee in this publication, or anywhere else for that matter, that your Christmas collectibles will increase in value. The best investment you can make is in your own education. The more you know about your collection and the hobby, the more informed the decisions you will be able to make.

We're not selling investment tips. We're offering ways to help you get the most enjoyment out of a rewarding hobby. If those rewards are monetary, great. But, above all, collecting should be fun.

So now, as Christmas approaches once again, prepare to enjoy this special time of year in the pages of this book — and in your own collection.

Celebrating 25 Years of Hallmark Keepsake Ornaments

By Meredith J. DeGood

Twenty-five years ago Hallmark Cards, Inc., issued 18 ornaments and launched a revolution in decorating Christmas trees.

The offering comprised six blown-glass ball ornaments and 12 yarn ornaments. The ball ornaments boast delightful bands decorated with Christmas scenes. One portrays a manger scene, another "Christmas is Love," and two feature Santa and his elves. The two others depict a little girl Hallmark called Betsey Clark.

The ball ornaments soon captured the hearts of Christmas collectors, and today the 1998 Keepsake line has 223 different ornaments with all types of materials designed to to fit the needs of all collectors.

Even as early as 1974 Hallmark researchers recognized the value of licensed properties in the line with the introduction of Raggedy Ann and Raggedy Andy. Mickey Mouse and his friends made their debut on Keepsake Ornaments in 1977, as did the Peanuts' gang. Many other popular properties have joined the Hallmark Keepsake Ornaments over the years.

As more artists joined the Hallmark design team, the Keepsake line expanded into series and more dates appeared on the ornaments. Soon collectors were asking for special ornaments for mother, father and other family members. Baby's First Christmas was commemorated with a ball ornament in 1976, and 1979 marked the introduction of a hand-crafted, hand-painted figural Baby's First Christmas ornament, and one or more in the series have been produced each year since.

In 1977, First Christmas Together was created for newlyweds and continues today. Soon after, other popular

series followed: Here Comes Santa Claus in 1979, the Rocking Horse in 1981 and the Tin Locomotive in 1982. Beginning in 1992, collectors could even commemorate their special relationships with their pets. A year later, Barbie fans saw their first ornament,

Holiday Barbie, and in 1994, Hallmark wheeled out the first edition in the Kiddie Car Classics series.

A major turning point in Keepsake collecting occurred in 1983, when Clara Johnson Scroggins authored her first Hallmark Keepsake Ornament

book (her seventh edition was published in early 1998). Until the first edition of the illustrated guide, people thought they had the entire collection of Hallmark ornaments only to find pictures in the first book of ones they did not know existed. Remember, that was before the days of home computers and the Hallmark annual "Dream Books," so Clara's book opened up a whole new world of Keepsake ornaments. Naturally, the popularity of the ornaments grew as scores of serious and casual collectors discovered pieces they just had to have.

In 1984 Hallmark added light to some ornaments, and as the years passed, voices, music and motion became quite popular. In 1990 the addition of on and off switches gave people the option of not having all these ornaments performing at the same time.

In 1987, in response to demand, Hallmark unveiled the Keepsake Ornament Collector's Club, today the largest ornament collector's club in the nation with an active membership of 250,000. Members receive a newsletter, special ornaments and the opportunity to purchase three other exclusive ornaments, and the chance to attend a host of special events, such as artist signings.

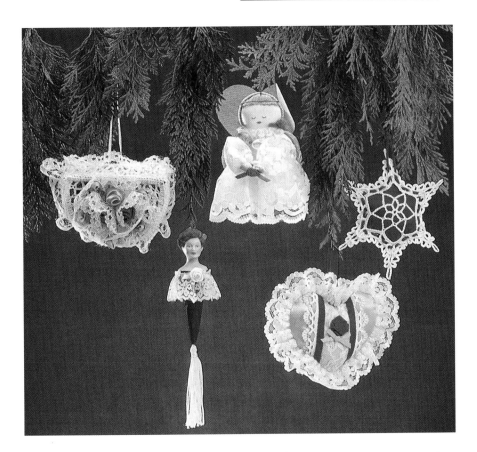

As lifestyles changed and more people were moving to smaller living areas, Hallmark created the Miniature Ornament line in 1988. Each year artists create intricate tiny ornaments approximately 1-1/2 inches in height for smaller trees, and in 1998 the famous Betsy Clark was slated to first appear in a miniature design.

Series of popular ornaments produced in relatively small numbers can enhance collectibility and, consequently, the value of the collectibles. Keepsake Ornaments serve as a perfect example of this. But keep in mind that collecting ornaments for only monetary gain can be risky. For one thing, although Hallmark never gives out production numbers, it seems apparent that the ornaments of the 1990s have been produced in much larger quantities than those of the late 1970s and early 1980s.

The ornaments made in the late 1980s and 1990s will probably never show such a phenomenal growth in secondary market values as the ones of earlier years. It is much better to purchase ornaments for your enjoyment and to commemorate special family achievements or milestones. Therefore, my advice is to purchase ornaments you like. It makes decorating your tree much more meaningful as you remem-

ber, why, where, when, or what prompted each purchase. Your tree then becomes a true Christmas symbol depicting your uniqueness.

Sometimes an ornament can rise sharply during the first year of release

and tumble in value over the following years. Such was the case with the 1986 Magical Unicorn, a hand-painted fine porcelain piece ($27.50 issue price, No. QX4293). Just 24,700 were produced, and everyone was searching for

a Magical Unicorn in 1986 and even in 1987. Stories circulated of early sales on this ornament of $175 to $250. But, as time has shown on many secondary market sheets, you could easily purchase one in 1998 for $30 to $50. Rumors of soaring prices and very limited supply had created a deceptive early market, and the predicted $500 value was never realized.

In contrast to the Unicorn, the two longest running series in the Hallmark Keepsake line are Here Comes Santa, in its 20th year, and Frosty Friends, in its 19th year. In 1979 Hallmark introduced Santa's Motorcar for $9.00. It was the first to be packaged with a decorative snow scene in the back of the box, and it was not listed as a series ornament until the following year. It is perhaps the most popular ornament ever produced by Hallmark. Today it still sells, Mint in the original box, for $650 to $700. One reason for the high value is that in the early 1980s Hallmark sold storage boxes in two sizes: for 36 or 48 ornaments. Since this seemed like an ideal way to keep a collection, people discarded many of the early ornament boxes since it was the ornaments, not the boxes, being collected. That's why it's difficult to locate a Mint-in-box 1979 item.

Another ornament that has held its substantial value is the 1980 A Cool Yule, which retailed for $6.50. It was

not announced as a series until the second year, and the series was titled Frosty Friends.

A Cool Yule depicts an Eskimo child and a polar bear friend holding song books and singing Christmas carols while sitting on an acrylic ice cube, which is captioned "Merry Christmas 1980." Many collectors do not know that the books are cardboard and were glued on. There are counterfeits of the books, and this piece is practically worthless with the false books. In Mint condition, and in a perfect box, this ornament sells for $750.

Another ornament that continues to

rise in popularity and price is the 1991 Starship Enterprise. Hallmark issued the lighted ornament to commemorate the 25th anniversary of the television series "Star Trek," and the detailed craft carries its identification, "U.S.S. Enterprise," and "NCC-1701" is repeated in several places. Issued for $20, it fetches $395 on the secondary market because of its popularity and scarcity.

Certainly, it's nice if your ornaments appreciate in value. That only adds to your enjoyment of the hobby. But the sure way to get the most out of Christmas collecting is to focus on the main reason: preserving family memories.

Remember, enjoy your collection throughout the year. There are darling Easter ornaments and Merry Miniatures to collect for all the holidays. Ornaments lend a festive look as table decorations for Valentine's Day, Easter, July 4, Halloween and Thanksgiving. Anytime is a fun time to use your ornaments!

HALLMARK:
PRICE GUID

Values were full retail selling prices at the time of publication, but it should be noted that lower prices can be found through extensive shopping.

HALLMARK PRICE GUIDE

Here are 50 of the more active Hallmark ornaments on the secondary market. Values are based on sales observed and reported by Meredith DeGood, collector and secondary market dealer as co-owner of the collectibles shop, The Baggage Car.

Year	Stock Number	Ornament	Value
1973	250 XHD1102	Betsey Clark Glass Ball - First Edition	125.00
1974	250 QX1101	Angel Glass Ball	95.00
1975	350 QX1321	Nostalgia Joy	245.00
1975	350 QX1291	Nostalgia Santa and Sleigh	225.00
1975	250 QX1601	Adorable Raggedy Andy	250.00
1976	350 QX2111	Baby's First Christmas - Satin Dated Ball	150.00
1976	300 QX1771	Tree Treat Santa - Dated	175.00
1977	350 QX2642	Betsey Clark Glass Ball - Fifth Edition	450.00
1977	500 QX1815	Nostalgia - Nativity	175.00
1978	450 QX1443	Red Cardinal Clip-on	175.00
1978	250 QX1336	Thimble Series (Mouse) - First Edition	295.00
1978	800 QX1503	Angels - Twirl about decorating Christmas tree	350.00
1978	600 QX1463	Carrousel Series - First Edition	400.00
1979	900 QX1559	Here Comes Santa - First Edition - Santa's Motorcar	695.00
1979	800 QX1419	Snoopy and Friends - First Edition (Ice Hockey Holiday)	175.00
1979	800 QX1547	Baby's First Christmas (Stocking) - Handcrafted	175.00

1980	650 QX1374	Frosty Friends - First Edition - A Cool Yule	750.00
1980	2000 QX1584	Checking It Twice - Special Edition	225.00
1980	1500 QX1567	Heavenly Minstrel - Special Edition	395.00
1980	550 QX1381	Santa's Flight - First Tin Ornament	125.00
1981	900 QX4222	Rocking Horse - First Edition	650.00
1981	450 QX8135	Christmas in the Forest Glass Ball	165.00
1981	650 QX4302	Space Santa	145.00
1981	450 QX8015	Traditional - Black Santa	97.50
1982	1300 QX4603	Tin Locomotive - First Edition	695.00
1982	1000 QX5023	Rocking Horse (Black) - Second Edition	450.00
1982	700 QX3133	Holiday Wildlife - Cardinals - First Edition	375.00
1983	1300 QX4037	Here Comes Santa - Santa pumps railroad handcar - Fifth Edition	295.00
1983	700 QX4289	Porcelain Bear - Cinnamon - First Edition	90.00
1983	1300 QX4057	Miss Piggy	250.00
1983	450 QX2219	Christmas Wonderland Glass Ball	175.00
1984	600 QX3484	The Twelve Days of Christmas - First Edition	325.00
1984	1300 QX4481	Nostalgic Houses and Shops -	215.00
1985	1250 QLX7032	Chris Mouse Lighted - First Edition First Edition	85.00
1985	2250 QX4985	Spirit of Santa Claus - Special Edition	95.00

1986	1375 QX4033	Nostalgic Houses and Shops - Candy Shop - Third Edition	395.00
1986	750 QX4223	Reindeer Champs - Dasher - First Edition	150.00
1986	1300 QX4026	Mr. and Mrs. Claus - First Edition	99.00
1987	1150 QX4407	Joy Ride	125.00
1988	500 QX4074	Mary's Angels - Buttercup - First Edition	49.50
1989	875 QX4352	Crayola Crayon - First Edition	72.50
1991	3000 QLX7273	Salvation Army Band - Light, Motion and Music	95.00
1991	1275 QX4319	Classic American Cars - 1957 Corvette - First Edition	195.00
1991	2000 QLX7199	Starship Enterprise - Light - 25th Anniv. of Star Trek	395.00
1993	1475 QX5725	Holiday Barbie - First Edition	175.00
1994	1095 QX5433	The Wizard of Oz Collection - Dorothy & Toto	75.00
1994	995 QX5436	The Wizard of Oz Collection - The Scarecrow	45.00
1994	995 QX5443	The Wizard of Oz Collection - The Tin Man	45.00
1994	995 QX5446	The Wizard of Oz Collection - The Cowardly Lion	45.00
1995	1295 QX5077	A Celebration of Angels - First Edition	40.00

Kiddie Car Classics

Hallmark introduced this collectible in 1992 through a division called Galleries. They are scale models of the popular sidewalk toys of the 1950s and '60s and are collected by many as memorabilia of their childhood. Kiddie Car Classics are sold in Hallmark Gold Crown Stores. This red-hot collectible may be cooling a bit due to the larger production numbers and the frequency with which they are being produced. In 1998 there were six new models for Father's Day in June and six more appeared in September. There is a companion piece, a Corner Drive-In, scheduled to arrive in late fall. It is numbered and the edition size is 39,500. Finally, in November through the Hallmark Gold Crown Catalog-Store Exclusive, the company began offering the 1930 Spirit of Christmas Custom Biplane for $65.00. Some collectors are backing off and not purchasing every new design.

Here are the top 15:

Year		Name	Stock Number	Edition Size	Current Value
1992	1955	Murray Fire Truck (Red/Yellow)	5000QHG9001	14,500	$450.00
1992	1941	Murray Airplane	5000QHG9003	14,500	450.00
1992	1955	Murray Tractor/ Trailer (Red)	5000QHG9004	14,500	395.00
1992	1955	Murray Champion (Blue)	4500QHG9008	14,500	375.00
1992	1953	Murray Dump Truck (yellow)	4800QHG9012	14,500	295.00
1993	1968	Murray Boat Jolly Roger	5000QHG9005	19,500	135.00
1994	1941	Steelcraft Spitfire Airplane	5000QHG9009	19,500	185.00
1994	1939	Steelcraft Lincoln Zephyr	5000QHG9015	24,500	135.00
1994	1955	Murray Firetruck	5000QHG9010	19,500	345.00
1995	1937	Steelcraft Auburn	6500QHG9021	24,500	195.00
1995	1960	Murray Torpedo	5000QHG9020	Open Edition	195.00
1993	1955	Murray Fire Chief	4500QHG9006	19,500	145.00
1994	1855	Murray Red Champion	4500QHG9002	19,500	175.00
1996	1935	Steelcraft Airplane, Air Mail	5000QHG9032	29,500	175.00
1997	1938	Garton Lincoln Zephyr	6500QHG9038	24.500	175.00

THE GLISTENING TREASURES OF BLOWN GLASS

BY MELANIE BENHAM

For centuries people have celebrated Christmas by decorating trees — first with festive cookies, candies, gilded fruits and nuts and then later in the mid- to late 1800s with blown glass. By 1998 Christmas ornaments have become the No. 1 collectible on the market today! Not everyone collects other items such as baseball cards, porcelain figurines, teddy bears, dolls or stamps. But virtually everyone collects ornaments in some manner. Many collectors make purchases based on production runs and the secondary market. Others focus on a specific line, theme, artist or company. But we all buy ornaments to commemorate the purchase of a new home, a wedding or anniversary, or to celebrate a new addition to the family, graduation or birthday. Your ornament collection is a tangible diary of your life.

Ornaments come in every shape, form and media. They are as whimsical as a plastic Santa from the 1950s, as cuddly as a tiny plush reindeer, as elegant as a Victorian scrap angel with tinsel, as traditional as a papier-maché German Belsnickle, or as futuristic as a talking metal robot. Modern technology has brought us mold-injected plastics and resins that can be manufactured in enormous quantities at relatively cheap prices.

However, it is the beautiful contemporary ornaments hand-blown and hand-painted in the centuries-old traditions that evoke cherished memories of a bygone era. These glistening treasures, ablaze with the reflection of thousands of tiny lights, spark the magic of Christmases past, present and future.

CHRISTOPHER RADKO

Since the mid-1980s Christopher Radko's name has been synonymous with Christmas. This is one man who has turned a tragedy into a triumph. One Christmas during his youth the inevitable happened. The family's 14-

foot tree toppled over, shattering all the breathtaking heirloom ornaments his ancestors had collected for generations.

That event was undoubtedly Christopher's destiny. When he tried to purchase new ornaments to replace his family's decorations, Christopher quickly discovered that cheap machine-made molded plastics had replaced the delicate hand-blown glittery figures from his childhood. Some time later while visiting relatives in Europe, Christopher had the good fortune to visit a tiny glass-blowing shop. Thus began the dazzling Radko ornament line in 1985.

There was not much activity on the secondary market for any glass orna-

ment line in the '80s and early '90s. The Radko organization debuted its Starlight Family of Collectors club in the winter of 1992. This was a big boost to the collectibilty of the line. Angels We Have Heard On High was the first members' only ornament. It issued for $50 and was limited to 5000 pieces. A Mint-in-box piece today will bring $350-$500 on the secondary market.

The most significant turning point in making the ornaments prized collectibles came in 1995 when Radko published his 10-year anniversary book with photos of almost every piece ever offered in his line. "The First Decade 1986-1995," commonly referred to as "the big book," is a Radko collector's

bible. Prior to its publication few collectors had copies of Radko's early catalogs so they simply did not know what to look for. The book enabled them to see all the ornaments they needed to add to their collections.

Through the big book, collectors discovered Radko began his first series — the Twelve Days of Christmas — in 1993. As collectors scrambled to locate the first two pieces in the series, the value of the Partridge In A Pear Tree ornament (which was issued for $33) skyrocketed to more than $1,600. Secondary market value for this piece has leveled off to a very respectable $850-$900. Most retailers threw away the white paper box in which the piece

had been shipped. If you find one with the original box, expect to pay an additional $50-$100.

Avid Radko collectors are usually on the trail of pre-1992 designs — especially very early pieces such as the Twin Finial, Double Royal Star, and Royal Star Finial. It is difficult to locate a Mint condition 1990 Ballooning Santa. This beautiful Victorian-style wire-wrapped ornament frequently has loose or broken wires. One in Mint condition will easily bring $200.

One of the more recent designs con-sistently performing well on the secondary market is the 1993 Santa Tree, which originally sold for $66. If you can locate one, expect to pay at least $350-$400 for a Mint Santa Tree. Similar designs that are equally popular are the Tree on Ball and Jumbo Tree on Ball.

Radko has no doubt revived the extraordinary tradition of the Czechoslovakian glass garland industry when he added the line in 1992. The whimsical 1993 Jack and Jill garland retailed for $41 and sells for over $150 in today's market.

In 1993 Radko began offering the distinctive free-blown Italian orna-ments.The extraordinary skill and additional time required to free-blow glass results in far lower production numbers and, consequently, enhances their col-lectibility. One Small Leap issued for $26 in 1993 and now sells in the $200 range. The eclectic Party Hopper sold for $33 in 1994. A legitimate Radko Party Hopper, (watch for knockoffs from other manufacturers), will fetch up to $300 on the secondary market.

Two years later, 1995, marked the beginning of the collaboration of

Radko and Disney with the introduction of two limited-edition designs. Mickey's Tree and Pooh's Favorite Gift were limited to 2,500 pieces each and retailed for $45. Initial secondary market prices for each piece soared to more than $300. Pooh's Favorite Gift continues to perform better than Mickey's Tree. Both are available today in the $100-$150 range. A signed Pooh will bring more than $200.

There have been many Radko/Disney pieces since, but most were produced in unlimited quantities and do not command the prices of the first two limited designs.

In 1996 Radko launched a new ornament series called the St. Nick Portrait series with an extremely limited design (750 pieces) called Esquire Santa. St. Nick Portrait series ornaments can be purchased only through Radko's premier Rising Star and Starlight stores. The issue price for a single Esquire ornament was a whopping $150. Even so collectors snapped these up as fast as they could. The Esquire initially brought $850-$1200 on the secondary market. However, when the production number for Regency Santa, the second piece in the series, was raised to 2,500, interest in the series dwindled. Esquire Santa can currently be obtained in the $500-$700 range.

OLD WORLD CHRISTMAS

The story of Tim and Beth Merck, president and premier designer of Old World Christmas, began in 1975. In an effort to attract customers to their antique furniture store during the holiday season, the young couple, who both speak German, decided to travel to Germany in search of the heirloom ornaments Beth recalled from her grandmother's tree.

The Mercks met members of the Inge-Glas company at the Nuremberg Toy show. Heinz and Klaus Müeller-Blech offered to take them to their fac-

tory to see the antique molds. On a dark and rainy night, the couple rode through the countryside to Coburg, Germany, where Beth selected 24 molds and Heinz blew them for her. Another family member silvered the ornaments and Beth painted them.

The rest, as they say, is history. For many years, all Old World Christmas ornaments were made from the "treasure trove" of antique molds using Beth's color schemes with more vibrant modern lacquers and colored glitters. Even with a repertoire exceeding 5,000 antique molds, Beth enjoys creating

new molds for the collectors of the 1990s.

One of the hallmarks of this line is the fabulous array of clip-on and hanging bird ornaments. In the early 1990s the Mercks encountered a man from a small German village who had a very old machine that was used to create all the spun glass for ornaments that Woolworth's sold in 1905! Beth then designed a wonderful assortment of ornaments with spun glass tails.

In 1996 Old World Christmas debuted a premier line of ornaments called the Birgit Collection. These fea-

ture larger and more intricate ornaments and proved to be very popular with collectors.

There is not a strong secondary market for Old World Christmas ornaments perhaps because they are so plentiful and affordable. One exception is the Charlie Chaplin ornament. Though this was an antique mold, apparently the descendents of Charlie Chaplin had some concerns about an ornament depicting their ancestor. The ornament was pulled from the line; however, a few had already been shipped. It retailed for $25 and continues to sell in

the $40-$50 range.

The company continues to produce some of the most exquisite Victorian designs on the market using paper-scrap figures, mini papier-maché wire wraps, metallic gold Dresden papers, chenille and other trims. For classic elegance at an affordable price you cannot beat the excellent value of Old World Christmas ornaments.

POLONAISE COLLECTION

The Kurt S. Adler company has supplied generations of Americans with every shape and form of lights, ornaments, stockings, garlands, party favors, figurines and tinsel. Ever the entrepreneur, Kurt S. Adler launched a premier line of collectible ornaments in 1994 called the Polonaise Collection.

The renowned Komozja family in Poland handcrafts the Polonaise ornaments using a heavier glass than most blown contemporary ornaments. The Komozja artists are able to carve extraordinary detail into their molds because of the weightier glass. This level of detail allows the artists to create award-winning designs such as the extraordinary MGM Studios-licensed Wizard of Oz pieces, Betty Boop and the new Titanic ornament.

Though Polonaise ornaments are known for their excellent quality and originality, they do not perform as well as some other ornament lines on the secondary market. This is most likely due to high production numbers. For example, beginning in 1994 one ornament in the Twelve Days of Christmas series has been released every year. To date none has been retired, so all five ornaments in this series are still available from retailers. An unlimited supply translates into limited demand from collectors.

Still, some Polonaise ornaments are active on the secondary market. The

1994 designs that were retired the first year of production are the prized possessions of many collectors. The Polonaise Golden Rocking Horse sold for $28 and rose to as high as $120 before settling in at about $60.

If luck is on your side and you locate one of the rare White Dice with the

designs. Disney and Adler terminated their licensing agreement mid-production, but about 1,000 Mickeys and 2,600 Minnies had already been shipped to retailers. With the crossover appeal from both Disney and ornament collectors for these $27 pieces, prices quickly eclipsed $200 for the set.

Patricia Breen Designs ornaments. Otherwise, you may never even have heard of the small Polish studio that produces the hottest collectible ornaments on the market today!

Breen ornaments quietly entered the U.S. market in 1994 at just a handful of retailers. As collectors spread

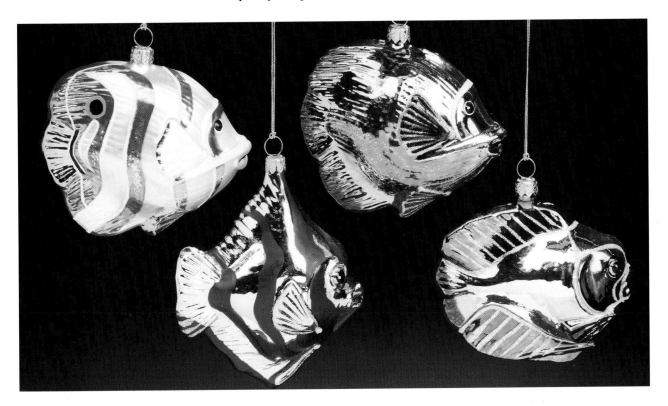

square corners, don't roll this die! It issued for $18 and currently sells in the $35-$40 range. The White Dice design was quickly retired because of difficulties in production and a high incidence of breakage, as square corners create stress points on the glass.

The hands down best performing Polonaise ornaments are the 1996 Mickey Mouse and Minnie Mouse

Today you can purchase the set for around $100-$125.

PATRICIA BREEN DESIGNS

Had you subscribed to one of the glass ornament newsletters in the past three years, you would be familiar with

word about the beautiful creations of Patricia and her husband, Eric Shaikewitz, an explosion rocked the blown-glass market in 1995.

"Location, location, location" drives the real estate market. For Patricia Breen Designs, the key to success is precision, precision, precision! This husband and wife team works side by side in its studio/factory in Poland cre-

ating their own original designs. Their ornaments are renown for attention to detail and precise application of custom-mixed lacquers and fine diamond dust glitters. Yet with all this attention to detail, Breen and Shaikewitz allow their artists some creative freedom in the painting and glittering of their designs.

The result is often a prized variant that can bring top dollar on the secondary market. Today there are fewer than 40 Breen retailers in the United States, and the studio has absolutely no plans for expansion. There are generally 50 to 60 new designs and 15 to 20 recolorations introduced each year. Many Breen collectors order the entire line sight unseen in September or October and hope to obtain the choice pieces by Christmas of the following year. Avid Breen collectors try to obtain every coloration of their favorite designs.

The hallmark of this line are the exquisite Santa figures, which have been known to skydive, fly beneath the moon, perch atop a computer monitor, pop out of a conch shell — even jettison to a galaxy far away with an alien co-pilot. Patricia Breen Designs also pioneered their trademark two-part ornaments. There are two types. The

first type has a companion ornament attached to a larger ornament through a loop pin. The Beeskep and Bee and Balloon Boy are very popular pieces produced in this fashion.

The second type is invariably one of most desirable design styles. This is where the second ornament is actually suspended from an annealed glass hook on the first ornament. The Goodnight Santa, Night Flight Santa and the whimsical Humbert are some of the most popular designs produced in this manner.

Collectors have a penchant for the extremely limited Fine Arts series ornaments. These are some of the most complex designs in the Breen line. They are produced in quantities of just 500-750 pieces. The attention to detail in the carving of the mold and in the intricate painting produces works of art that can truly be called masterpieces. The Fine Arts series is in its fourth year and includes St. George and the Dragon, Blow Gabriel Blow, St. Peter, and Joan of Arc.

Expect to pay $200-$500 or more

for an ornament in Mint condition from the 1994 and early 1995 lines if you can locate one. It is quite common for a store-exclusive coloration to sell for $30-$60, and less than a month later that same ornament will bring five to 10 times the issue price on the secondary market. A recent charity auction for a one-of-a-kind gold coloration of the Breen Miniature Santas (set of three) garnered a record $1,479 bid!

The Breen studio defines collectibilty by maintaining the utmost in detail in their products as well as producing truly limited editions. Each ornament is produced in quantities ranging from 500 to 2,000. This essentially makes every ornament a limited edition. A mold may be painted in several colorations. However, the total number of pieces made from a mold is always 2,000 or less. The result is museum quality pieces that are destined to become family heirlooms.

The issue prices provided in this article will vary slightly from retailer to retailer across the country. Secondary market price ranges quoted herein have been taken from actual sales from 1996 through 1998. Collectors could expect to pay more or less depending on the condition of the ornament, region of the country, time of the year and whether the ornament has its original tag. (Old World Christmas ornaments generally do not have tags.) In most cases ornaments are not sold in a box. However, when they did come packaged, the box itself and condition of the box will also affect value.

Today's collectible ornaments are the antiques of tomorrow. If you are purchasing for investment, remember condition is the prime factor that determines value. Check each piece for scratches, paint chips, missing glitter, hanger scratches and mildew spots. Proper storage is the key to maintaining the condition of your pieces. Never leave ornaments locked in a hot car. Do not store your collection in an attic or basement. Protect your ornaments by storing them in a climate-controlled room wrapped in acid-free tissue instead of bubble wrap. And by all means insure your collection!

Surely one of the nicest things about ornaments is that no matter how you choose to display them they look fantastic. They are not just for Christmas anymore. Contemporary designers now offer exceptional lines for spring, Easter, Fourth of July, autumn and even Halloween! Whether you are collecting ornaments for investment or pure enjoyment, have fun with your collection. Proudly display your best 25-cent yard sale find with your most cherished collectible ornament. Create theme trees, topiaries with glass fruit or glittering mantle piece swags. Share the Christmas spirit by giving ornaments to friends. Most importantly, remember the Christmas spirit is contagious. Catch it and pass it on!

BLOWN GLASS: PRICE GUIDE

Values were full retail selling prices at the time of publication, but it should be noted that lower prices can be found through extensive shopping.

BLOWN GLASS ORNAMENT PRICE GUIDE

These are the most popular blown-glass ornaments at retail and/or on the secondary market from 1996 to mid-1998. The "Value Range" for the secondary market reflects actual sales.

Christopher Radko

Order No.	Ornament	Retail Price	Value Range
86-005-0	Candy Cane	6	50-75
86-010-0	Snow Comet	15	75-100
86-023-0	Saturn	5	50-75
86-040-0	Alpine Flowers	12	35-50
87-010-0	Scarlett's Wedding Dress	14	50-75
87-034-0	Faberge	27	120-150
87-038-0	Serpents	6	20-25
87-079-0	Double Royal Star	20	90-150
87-080-0	Twin Finial	20	90-150
88-064-0	Tree On Ball	9	125-225
88-080-0	Royal Star Tree Top	25	175-250
89-030-0	Fleurs-de-Provence	17	75-100
89-054-0	Seahorse-coral	10	100-125
89-061-3	A Shy Rabbit's Heart	15	60-90
89-104-0	His Boy Elroy	8	100-120
89-108-0	Royal Star Finial	42	225-325
90-003-0	Poinsettia	18	100-125
90-058-0	Frog Under Balloon	14	75-100
90-087-0	Ballooning Santa	20	175-225
90-101-0	Jumbo Tree On Ball	30	150-250
91-020-0	Evening Santa	15	100-125

91-038-0	Woodland Santa	14	50-75
91-052-0	Sleepytime Santa	15	50-75
91-075-E	Forever Lucy	32	45-60
91-076-0	Aspen	21	45-65
91-094-0	Ms. Maus	14	100-150
91-112-1	Santa in Winter White(white hat)	28	125-150
91-137-0	All Weather a Santa/Umbrella Sant	32	125-150
92-175-0	Floral Cascade Tier Drop	32	90-125
92-185-0	Benjamin's Nutcracker set of pink and blue	116	225-275
92-208-0	Gold Link Chain Garland	16	60-75
93-021-0	Sterling Reindeer	113	350-500
93-085-0	Jack n Jill Garland	41	125-200
93-127-0	Santa in Space	39	90-125
93-143-0	Fantasia	24	50-75
93-221-0	Tutti Frutti carrot	26	40-50
93-222-0	One Small Leap	26	150-250
93-224-0	Centurian	26	125-175
93-243-0	Crystal Fountain	34	100-125
93-253-0	Emperor's Pet	22	150-250
93-284-0	Ice Bear	18	35-50
93-308-0	Crystal Rainbow	30	150-200
93-320-0	Santa Tree	66	325-450
93-SP1	Angels We Have Heard On High	50	350-500
93-SP2	Partridge In A Pear Tree	33	800-1000
94-278-0	Swan Fountain	44	125-150
94-SP3	Starbuck Santa	75	225-300
94-SP4	Two Turtle Doves	28	100-150

94-SP5	Frosty Cares	25	45-60
95-026-0	Frog Lady	24	35-50
95-076	South Bend Polar Express	27	50-75
95-192-0	Sweet Madame	48	125-150
95-DIS-1	Mickey's Tree	45	150-200
95-DIS-2	Pooh's Favorite Gift	45	175-225
95-NC01	Nutcracker Suite One	90	85-100
95-SP09	Three French Hens	34	60-100
96-SP12	Four Calling Birds	44	50-80
96-SP17	Esquire Santa	150	500-700
97-SP19	Five Gold Rings	62	60-90
97-SP24	Regency Santa	175	175-200

Old World Christmas

Order No.	Ornament	Retail Price	Value Range
1202	Playing Cat	9	10
1206	Sitting Dog With Pipe	8	11
1493	Large Santa In Chimney (club)	43	80
1512	'94 Santa In Moon	33	40

	On Disc (ltd. edition)		
1550	Flying Peacock With Wings (ltd. edition)	23	24
1615	Large Parrot on Ball	11	12
1811	Lilac Bird	9	10
1816	Snow Owl	10	14
1825	Miniature Peacock	8	13
2001	Gingerbread House	7	16
2011	Garden House with Gnome	8	14
2023	Large Lighthouse Mill	11	11
2409	Clown With Accordion	10	11
2426	Mr. Big Nose	8	19
2470	Clown Above Ball	42	45
2487	Charlie Chaplain	25	40-50
3010	Heart With Flowers	10	13
131	O' Tannenbaum	35	35
133	Old Christmas Barn	50	50
141	Guarding My Children	65	65

Polonaise

Order No.	Ornament	Retail Price	Value Range
GP	Szlackic 1996 signing event piece	35	40-45
GP312	Snowman with Glasses	20	30-40
GP332	Parrot	14	30-40
GP339	Apple	10	30-40
GP347	Gnome	18	50-60
GP355	Gold Rocking Horse	18	60-75
GP363	White Dice	18	40-60
GP372	Angel Head	18	90-150
GP373	Merlin	18	25-35
GP390	Cat with Ball	16	25-35
GP391	Minnie Mouse	27	40-50
GP392	Mickey	27	75-125
GP396	Angel With Bear	18	30-50
GP397	Brontosaurus	20	30-50
GP420	Cardinal	18	30-50
GP422	Silver Puppy	16	60-75
GP448	Telephone	20	20-30
GP500	Egyptian Collection 12 pc. Set	195	200-250
GP502/4	Roman set of 4	100	85-100
GP508	Wizard Of Oz 6 pc. Boxed set	150	150-200

Patricia Breen Designs

Ornament	Retail Price	Value Range
A Snack For Rudolph dark purple	35	50-90
Amor Angel	35	60-100
Archimbaldi	60	160-250
Balloon Boy red glitter balloon	40	80-120
Balloon Boy red glitter balloon w/green tree	45	100-150
Balloon Boy red/green glitter diamond balloon	45	150-250
Beaux Art FaÁade	45	150-175
Beeskep & Bee	30	60-90
Bijoux Santa purple	55	95-125
Blow, Gabriel, Blow	75	120-180

Chocolate Box Santa bordeaux	35	60-75	Night House	35	75-90
Classic Tree	25	90-125	Oak Leaf Santa gold	45	40-60
Dish And Spoon blue	30	60-75	Oak Leaf Santa orange	45	75-90
Faberge Santa blue glitter	35	70-80	Queen of Hearts blue glitter heart	35	100-125
Faberge Santa green glitter	35	450-600	Queen of Hearts red glitter heart	35	40-50
Faberge Santa red glitter	35	225-250	Rocket Boy	20	90-110
Faberge Santa red paint	35	75-100	Snowman	20	45-60
Father Time light blue	30	125-175	Sojourning Santa	40	60-75
Frog King	30	40-55	Sojourning Santa pearl signing event	70	200-250
Henry, The Baby Bear	25	45-60	St. George and the Dragon	70	300-500
I Love You Santa	35	60-100	St. Peter	85	250-400
Icarus Flies	50	50-60	St. Petersburg Santa green	30	80-100
Lady Bug red	10	40-60	Striped Santa green/white	35	125-175
Light House Keeper blue	45	75-100	Striped Santa red/white	35	50-60
Lily Of the Valley Egg	50	125-150	Summer Acorn House	35	60-75
Love Is In The Air	55	60-75	Swell Starfish	30	60-75
Madonna for Pablo	80	90-125	Winter Acorn House	35	45-60
Making His List cobalt/gold trim	35	50-60	Winter Wizard	25	50-65
Moon and Many Stars cobalt	20	100-125	Woodland Santa bordeaux	40	60-75
Night Flight	60	100-150	Woodland Santa light blue	35	125-150

'Twas The Night Before Christmas

FIGURINES REPRESENT THE SPIRIT OF THE HOLIDAYS

By Dean A. Genth

ollectors yearn for symbols of Christmases when times were simpler and innocence was abundant. As our modern lifestyles become ever more harried and impersonal, many of us search for figurines and figure-shaped ornaments that reflect the best of Christmas — the joy, the beauty, and all things spiritual.

In response to collector demand for nostalgic Christmas-themed product, several manufacturers offer special Christmas memories in various forms. Figurines, ornaments, and houses seem to dominate the Christmas collectibles category.

Some manufacturers had their early beginnings as companies producing specifically for the Christmas market. One notable example is Possible Dreams with its Clothtique Santas. The company has expanded its line steadily during the past several years from a few Santas that were fairly traditional in style to a line of Santas that includes representations of occupations as well as playful themes. Collectors of Clothtique Santas can now find the likes of a doctor Santa, golfer Santa, fireman Santa and a policeman Santa.

Most figurine producers begin with a line of figurines that represents nostalgic images, but are general in theme. We can easily think of hundreds of popular figurines that depict children partaking of the simple joys of childhood in years past or of cute animals playing in a make-believe, pastoral setting. Even the companies that concentrate on non-holiday related images seem to release a substantial offering of Christmas figurines for collectors

annually.

In an effort to enhance the collectibiliy of their lines, some companies have begun to issue annual limited-edition Christmas pieces. Collectors seem to respond positively to the annual edition releases due to the fact that these items are limited to one year of production only. With that method of marketing comes the all-important sense of urgency on the part of the collector to make certain those pieces are obtained without delay.

Thus, Precious Moments has its annual Christmas figurine and ornament, Dept. 56 a limited edition annual building, Cherished Teddies an ornament and a figurine, M. I. Hummel its annual Christmas bell, and the list goes on and on. In order to understand the depth of Christmas collectibles that are available to collectors on the secondary market, let's take a closer look at the most actively traded lines of figurines on the retail and secondary markets. They are in alphabetical order: Boyd's Bears, Charming Tails, Cherished Teddies, Dept. 56, M.I. Hummel, Possible Dreams, Precious Moments and United Design.

BOYD'S BEARS

Boyd's Bears stands out from the crowded figurine world as being possibly the most nostalgic and emotionally driven in this competitive and richly diverse category. Collectors the world over are apt to excitedly tell you that the Boyd's Bears figurines are so cute, so adorable and so homey.

That arises from the indisputable

fact that all the products of The Boyds Collection Ltd. have been endowed with so much personality. This comes about due in part to the fact that they all are "born" with people names such as Bailey and Matthew. It just so happens that these are the names of the children of Gary Lowenthal and his wife, the creators of Boyd's. It is the Boyd's Nativity that seems to be generating the most interest among Boyd's collectors when we think of leading Boyd's Christmas-themed releases. The Boyd's nativity was released over a period of several years and portrays the Boyd's Bear characters putting on the Christmas Nativity in "live" pageant form. This nativity is slated for retirement in 1999 and has the earmarks of a major player in the secondary market arena.

The Boyd's Bears lines encompass more than 600 styles from 3-inch miniatures to 21-inch cuddly giants. Most notable is the Bearstone Collection with Bailey, Matthew and the gang, but collectors don't overlook the whimsical folk art of the figurines, Santas, angels and hares in the Folkstone Collection.

CHARMING TAILS

Charming Tails created by Dean Griff are noteworthy woodland critters who take their collectors on a nostalgic and fun ride to woodland retreats such as the now-famous Squashville where fun and fantasy combine to whisk us away from present day concerns. Fitz & Floyd distributes the Charming Tails figurines and ornaments, which go by irrestible names such as Mackenzie and Maxine Mouse, Binkey and Bunnie Bunny, Chauncey Chipmunk and Reginald Raccoon.

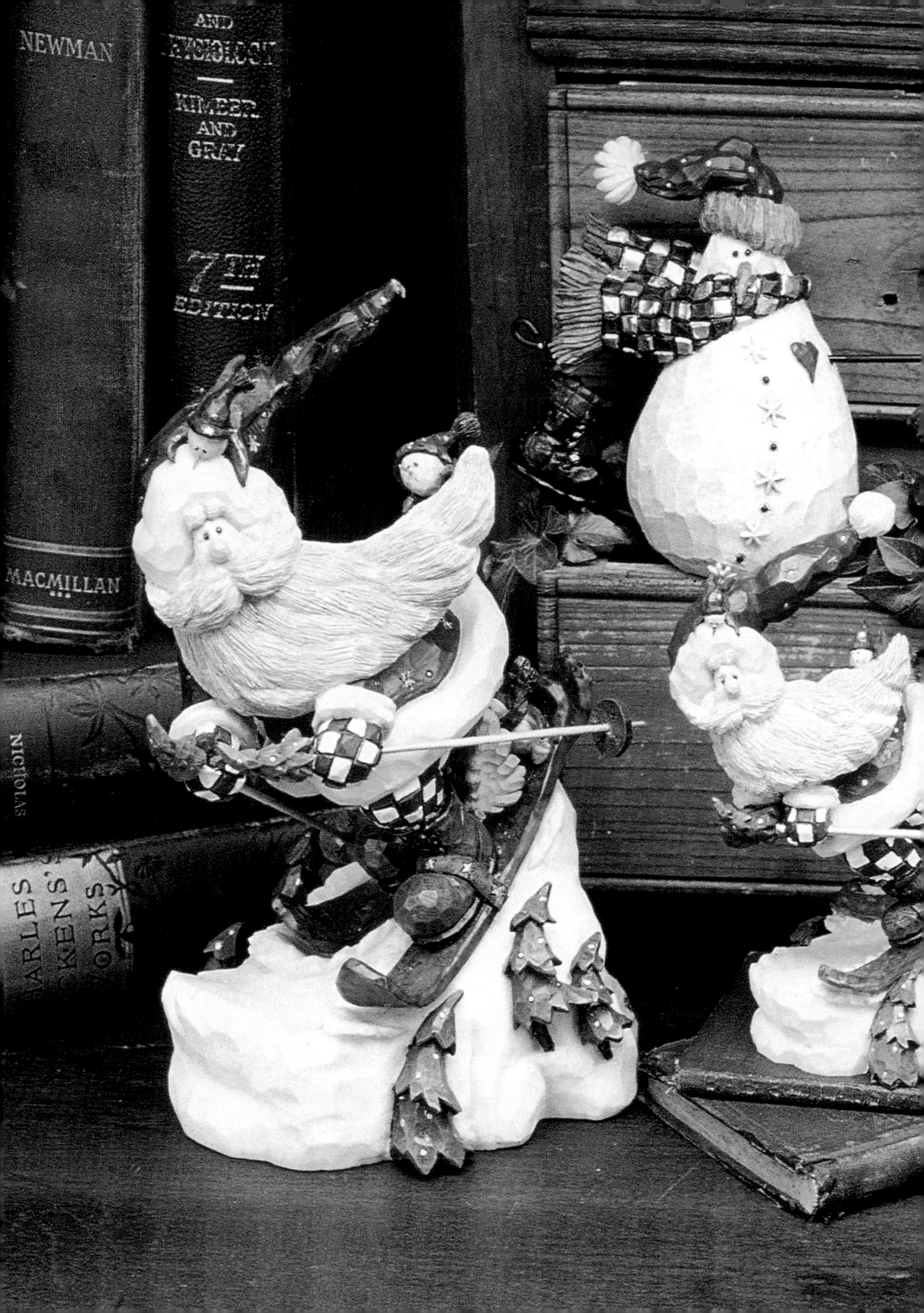

Griff's imagination and creativity have created a line of figurines that causes collectors to want many or most of every piece he has created. One of the many strengths of this line that gives it strong secondary market appeal is the rapid pace of retirements. With frequent retirements the Charming Tails line is continually fresh and exciting.

The top two Charming Tails with a Christmas theme are Sleigh Ride, retired in 1995, and the limited-edition (7,500 pieces) Mackenzie Building a Snowmouse. Sleigh Ride sells today for $125. Mackenzie Building a Snowmouse was issued in 1994 at $18 and now sells for $125.

CHERISHED TEDDIES

The Enesco Corporation distributes Cherished Teddies, by artist Priscilla Hillman. Collectors have a great love affair going with

Cherished Teddies evidenced by the many awards that Priscilla and Enesco have won with this line. Since there are so many Cherished Teddie collectors, increasing activity on the secondary market seems likely. The current interest seems to be settling around the 1993 Family on Toboggan, which has a current secondary market value of $195, and the 1993 Theodore, Samantha, and Tyler with a secondary market value of $160. Collectors of Cherished Teddies seem to seek especially the limited editions and specially released items.

DEPT. 56

Dept. 56 has become synonymous with villages and buildings that collectors adore, not only at Christmas time, but throughout the year.

The Original Snow Village and Dickens Village have been the two

main cornerstones of this popular collectible. Collectors of all walks of life are attracted to the idea of putting together their favorite village, fully lighted and properly executed with all the necessary accessories. After all, what would a village be without lampposts, street signs, trees and shrubs?

Two Dept. 56 items that have been top performers on the secondary market are not traditional houses. One of the most difficult-to-find Dept. 56 items is the Snowbabies piece entitled Frosty Frolic, #7981-2. The 1988 Frosty Frolic was limited to 4,800 pieces and currently commands $1,000 on the secondary market.

Another top performer is the 1992 Village Express Van, item #9977-5, Gold. The Village Express Van was a promotional item and as a retired piece commands $975 on the secondary market.

M.I. HUMMEL

The M. I. Hummel figurines are still hand-crafted by superbly skilled German artisans at the Goebel factory in Roedental Germany. The Hummel figurines are inspired by the artwork of Sister M.I. Hummel, who died in 1946 after the end of World War II of tuber-

cular pneumonia.

Since artist M.I. Hummel had sketched some drawings depicting children engaged in Christmas activities, several figurines have been produced with a holiday theme. Two of the most valuable Hummel figurines ever produced by Goebel break the bank in terms of Christmas collectibles. Due to the German political climate in the 1930s, Hum #31, Silent Night with Black Child, was never authorized to be mass-produced. Hummel #31 in a crown trademark has sold for as high as $20,000 on the secondary market.

Another very rare Christmas

ularity with collectors and selected new releases are often bought quickly by enthusiasts. Popular lines are the Clothtique Santas in the American Artist Collection and Signature Series, as well as the playful pieces of Crinkle Claus, cold-cast creations with distinctive wrinkled surfaces. There is not, however, a strong secondary market yet for Possible Dreams Santas.

PRECIOUS MOMENTS

The Precious Moments line by artist Sam Butcher is distributed by the Enesco Corporation. Spiritual inspiration is the guiding force of this line, so it is only natural that Christmas translates so well into the pieces. Precious Moments figurines are celebrating 20 years of inspiring the public with their wide-eyed children.

The line began in 1978 with the release of 21 porcelain bisque figures with inspirational messages, and by 1998, Butcher had created more than 1,000 different Precious Moments figures, many still in production.

Two of the most valuable Christmas items command impressive values and, naturally, are difficult to find in good

Hummel figurine is Letter to Santa in its original sample form. Hum #340 was first sculpted in 1956 by Helmut Wehlte and was not produced in mass quantities until 1972. The early sample pieces are valued at $15,000-$20,000. The early sample pieces would bear a "full bee" trademark.

POSSIBLE DREAMS

Possible Dreams produces the Santa figurines known by their trademark name, Clothtique. Although many companies have tried to copy this item, it is the Possible Dreams Clothtique pieces that collectors are seeking.

The uniqueness of Clothtique® comes from a blend of porcelain, stiffened cloth and resin, adorned with festive coloring. The 1991 Gramps with Reins sells for $290. Along with this piece was another 1991 release entitled Magic of Christmas that sells for $140 on the secondary market.

Possible Dreams Santas enjoy pop-

condition. Silent Night Musical, #E-5642, was issued for $45 and now lists in excess of $475. A very special Precious Moments Nativity is the hard-to-find special dealer Nativity, #104523. This limited production set commands a price in excess of $500.

UNITED DESIGN

United Design manufactures Christmas figurines annually in limited editions. The privately owned company was founded in 1973 and is the world's largest producer of animal-theme figurines.

In 1991, United Design produced The Gift, numbered AA-009, in a limited edition of 3,500 pieces. Issue price was $140, and The Gift now sells for $500. Santa with Pups, CF-003, is a 1986 release that debuted at $65, but now sells for $250.

With this overview of Christmas collectibles, one can see that the innocence of children and whimsy of cute animals, when blended with the wonder of Christmas, make for a collector's delight. So many choices abound for the figurine collector that one could collect only Christmas related products and be happy and busy for as long as they chose to pursue their hobby.

FIGURES: PRICE GUIDE

Values were full retail selling prices at the time of publication, but it should be noted that lower prices can be found through extensive shopping.

FIGURINE PRICE GUIDE

From 1996 to mid-1998, these have been the most popular items among figurines at retail and/or on the secondary market (in addition to the items cited the overview by Dean Genth).

Boyd's Bears

No.	Figure	Value
270501	Bailey, The Night Before Christmas	42
228310	S.C. Northstar & Emmett, Lil' Helper	26
228311	Edmund the Elf, Christmas Carol	16
2242	Elliott & Snowbeary	17
2240	Edmund & Bailey, Gathering Holly	26
228308	Guinvere the Angel, Love is the Master Key	16
2283	Kringle & Company	20
25953	Noel Bruinski, Da Electrician	14
25955	Serendipity, Peace to All	23
2243	Manheim, The Eco-Moose	17

Charming Tails

No.	Figure	Value
87/621	Who Put That Tree There?	17
87/510	Maxine Making Snow Angels	21
87/580	Binkey Snowshoeing	15
87/622	Merry Christmas From Our House to Yours	23
87/702	Trimming The Tree (2 piece)	28
87/623	Team Igloo	23
87/625	Please, Just Once More . . .	17
87/624	Dashing Through The Snow	17
86/658	Tricycle Built From Treats	13
86/659	Pine Cone Predicament	11

Cherished Teddies

No.	Figure	Value
951129	Steven-A Season Filled With Sweetness	97
912875	Alice	233

No.	Figure	Value
141100	Nickolas	77
950769	Theadore, Samantha and Tyler	160
950742	Charlie	93
141135	Meri	20
352386	Missy, Cookie & Riley	35
352799	Segrid, Justaf, & Ingmar	45
175986	Angela	20
354244	Keith & Deborah	30

M. I. Hummel

No.	Figure	Value
301	Christmas Angel	280
343	Christmas Song	245
2014	Christmas Delivery	485
396	Ride Into Christmas	485
755	Heavenly Angel Tree Topper	495
2002	Making New Friends	595

239/D	Girl With Fir Tree	60
357	Guiding Angel	100
83	Angel Serenade	245
188/0	Celestial Musician	245

Precious Moments

No.	Figure	Value
112401	I'm Sending You A White Christmas	145
109476	Peace on Earth	170
109754	Wishing You A Ymuuy Christmas	75
12351	Halo, and Merry Christmas	225
5641	They Followed the Star	250
455784	Alaska Once More, How's Yer Christmas	35
455822	I Saw Mommy Kissing Santa Claus	65
529273	My True Love Gave To Me	40
521884	Pizza On Earth	55
521507	The Light of the World is Jesus	70

Nutcrackers: Old-World Charmers

By Susan Ford Wiese

THE
ADRIAN TARON & SONS
COLLECTION

Tchaikovsky's
"Mouse King"

ORIGINAL
STEINBACH
VOLKSKUNST
GERMANY

High in the Erzgebirge region of Germany, close to the Czech border lies the picturesque village of Seiffen. This is Christmas town. Nutcrackers, pyramids, and carved etchings, bigger than life, decorate the outside of buildings and homes. Sidewalks illuminated by lanterns and windows lit by candles welcome visitors.

It is here in "Christmas Country" that the cottage crafts developed after the demise of the mining industry and the advent of the lathe. In the hearts of these people, live the stories of the miners and their handiwork, of legends and folklore. The economically successful toy industry began here and branched out through trade to Nuremberg, Europe, overseas and eventually into our homes. Even today, local artisans still work out of their homes using lathes and wheels. Several generations of a family assist in different aspects of the fine detail work. This is considered the home of the nutcracker.

In 1816, "The Nutcracker and the King of Mice," a beautiful and romantic fairy tale by E.T.A. Hoffmann, was published and introduced the nutcracker as a hero and enchanted prince. This was a forerunner to Tchaikovsky's "Nutcracker Suite." The famous ballet

probably inspired Wilhelm Friedrich Fuchtner. He was known as the father of the Seiffen nutcrackers and made them from tough material to withstand hard nuts and children's hands. His King nutcrackers are considered prototypes for Erzgebirge nutcrackers.

In the beginning, authority figures were used "to crack the hard nuts." The

common people enjoyed the irony of using kings, soldiers and policemen to do the work for them. These figures with their grim expressions, big teeth and sharp noses represented a social criticism of those who often were in charge of the people.

Traditional collections of nutcrackers consisted of a king, then his henchmen and guards. There might follow a cook, musicians and servants.

Today, nutcrackers come in every size and all varieties. Sizes range from nearly 7 feet to just a few inches, with the more popular ones ranging from about 5-1/2 to 17 inches. Series cover the spectrum: characters in the "Nutcracker Suite," U.S. presidents, legendary heroes such as King Arthur, fairy tale characters, Santas and snowmen. Even the Wizard of Oz graces

Dorothy

AMERICAN PRESIDENTS
Theodore Roosevelt
1858 ~ 1919

Great American Inventors

Alexander Graham Bell

mantelpieces and bookshelves.

STEINBACH

The Steinbach Company has been hand-crafting nutcrackers for five generations. Christian Steinbach, the 76-year-old president of the company based in the Erzgebirge region of Germany, is an astute showman. He tours the United States making personal appearances and signings. He intro-

Kurt Adler Company of New York, Merlin demands the highest price in the secondary market at about $4,000. In 1991, the $185 Merlin quickly sold out and was followed by King Arthur and the rest of the Camelot series. Since 1992, Kurt Adler has introduced several exclusive limited editions and most have sold out. Other series are Christmas Carol, Christmas Legends, and Tales of Sherwood Forest — both

Taron & Sons of Carpinteria, Calif., also commissions Steinbach exclusives. Their first nutcracker, 1992 Herr Drosselmeyer, Limited Edition (6,000), is the second highest seller on today's market at nearly $3,000. Currently there are six in the Nutcracker Suite Series with the edition of the Toy Soldier this year. In 1999, Taron plans to add a series of Chinese, Spanish and Russian Dancers. The Three Wisemen

duced the limited-edition nutcracker when he made exclusives for House of Tyrol, Westphal and others.

However, it was the Merlin the Magician, Limited Edition (7,500), that turned nutcrackers into coveted collectibles. Made by Steinbach for the

in standard size (17 inches) and minature (5-1/2 inches.) King Wenceslaus and Marek, his henchman, the first two Collector's Club pieces, continue the trend of limited editions with runs of 4,000 each.

The Taron Collection, from Adrian

is a handsome set, and both the full size and the miniature sets have proven popular on the retail market, with prices in the mid-$200 range.

Four years ago Steinbach miniatures (5-1/2 inches) appeared on the market and both Adler and Taron have intro-

Cowardly Lion

Great American Inventors
Henry Ford

THE CHRISTMAS LEGENDS
FATHER CHRISTMAS
~ 1850 ~

THE CHRISTMAS LEGENDS
ST. NICHOLAS
~ 1650 ~

duced exclusive lines. They currently sell in $50-$60 range. The Steinbach company also introduced a 12-inch chubby edition of their regular selections and they sell from $95-$120. This has opened up collecting to those who did not have room or the budget for the full size Steinbachs.

ULBRICHT

Christian Ulbricht is another famous German nutcracker maker. For many years his line was carried by several import firms, with exclusives and limited editions made for Midwest of Cannon Falls, Minn. The company has formed its own import company, Ulbricht USA, which has introduced several original and high-quality limited-edition nutcrackers.

Ulbricht's Santas have always been a favorite with their wonderful toys and gentle, benevolent features. Round noses, stains and careful attention to detail characterize the Ulbricht line. Christian also does signings and tours to promote his lines. Shakespeare, Wizard of Oz, Inventors, the Christmas Carol and Indians are new series selling well.

Though not as prevalent on the secondary market as Steinbach nutcrack-

ers, Ulbricht pieces are popular at the retail level. Two exceptions are sold out nutcrackers distributed by Midwest. The 1996 Teddybear Maker sold for $270 and now goes for $450, and the 1993 Father Christmas retailed for $210 and now moves for about $350.

Both Ulbricht's and Steinbach's original factories were in the Erzgebirge region in Seiffen and the

neighboring town, Marienberg. Following World War II, the German Democratic Republic confiscated and nationalized the factories and took over production. Steinbach and Ulbricht relocated their factories to West Germany, explaining why Erzgebirge nutcrackers with GDR stamps originated during this time. Because they were subsidized by the East German government, they were inexpensive and plen-

STEINBACH

KSA
COLLECTIBLES

*Merlin *
"The Magician"

ORIGINAL STEINBACH
VOLKSKUNST
GERMANY

*Merlin *
"The Magician"

tiful. Following the collapse of the Berlin Wall, the Steinbach and the Ulbricht families repurchased their old factories and resumed producing nutcrackers where their fathers did.

The nutcracker craft is rapidly returning to the Seiffen area as families adjust to capitalism. Nutcrackers coming from this region bear the town's name or family name. Lines can be distinguished from one another by family trademarks or details. Although more expensive than those from the Cold War era, many are still made in homes and hand-turned and painted.

MERCK AND MCDOWELL

Beth Merck, from Spokane, Wash., designs and markets the whimsical nutcrackers of Old World Christmas. Hand-crafted also in the Erzgebirge region, they have distinctive round bellies, wood mustaches, rabbit fur and wooden accessories. They fill a middle market between the generic Seiffen nutcrackers and the limited editions of Steinbach and Ulbricht.

Another North American artist from the Northwest — Vancouver, British Columbia, to be exact — is Sean McDowell, who makes 2- to 7-foot figures ideal for display or making a statement. He will also do custom work, as in Amadeus the Conductor, made for a Canadian orchestra. His 28-inch Mouse King is one of his best sellers. At the entrance of the Steinbach display at the Nuremberg Toy Fair stood a 7-foot McDowell King of the Nutcrackers . . . a tribute to a master.

Summer Wonderland

Nutcrackers: Price Guide

Values were full retail selling prices at the time of publication, but it should be noted that lower prices can be found through extensive shopping.

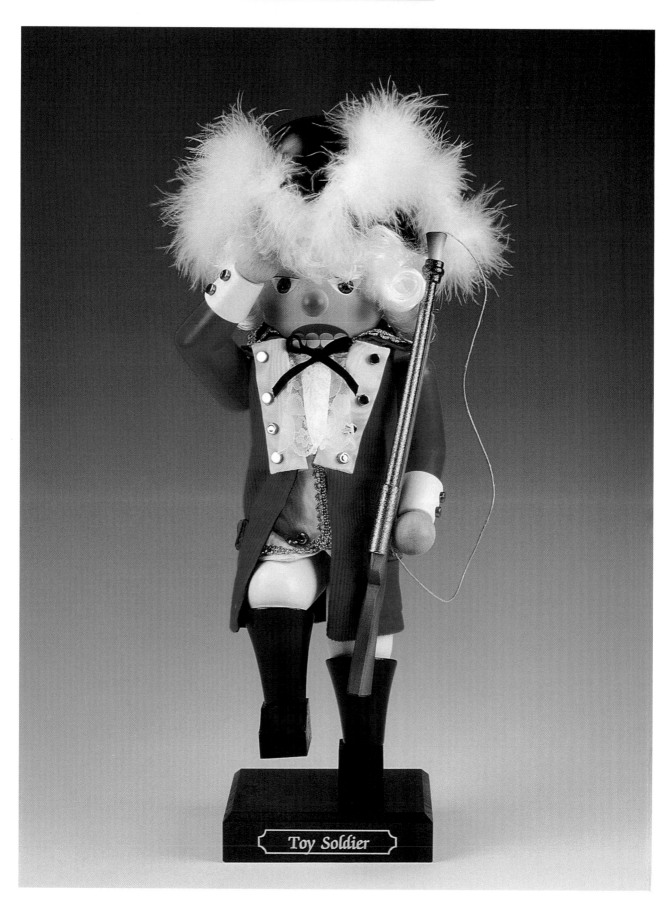

Toy Soldier

NUTCRACKER PRICE GUIDE

Here are the most popular nutcrackers at retail and/or on the secondary market. Values were reported selling prices, both retail and secondary market, at time of publication. Current retail prices for regular-size (about 17 inches) Steinbach and Ulbricht nutcrackers range from $210 to $240. Slightly smaller, standard Merck nutcrackers range from $145 to $199.

Steinbach

Kurt S. Adler

No.	Name	Issue Size	Issued-Retired	Value
ES610	Merlin	7500	1991-1991	3200-4200
ES621	King Arthur	12000	1992-1993	900-1200
ES869	Queen Guinevere	10000	1995-1997	300-400
ES862	Sir Lancelot	12000	1993-1997	300-400
ES638	Sir Galahad	12000	1994-1997	300-400
ES645	Father Christmas	7500	1993-1996	500-600
ES865	Saint Nicholas	7500	1993-1996	600
ES891	1930 Santa Claus	7500	1995-	260
ES895	Grandfather Frost	7500	1997-	260
ES1822	Pere Noel Santa	7500	1998-	260
ES637	Chief Sitting Bull	8500	1993-1995	500
ES864	Red Cloud	8500	1994-1996	325
ES889	Blackhawk	7500	1995-1996	325
ES863	Robin Hood	7500	1992-1996	600
ES890	Friar Tuck	7500	1995-1997	300
ES892	Sheriff of Nottingham	7500	1996-	260

No.	Name	Issue Size	Issued-Retired	Value
ES897	King Richard	7500	1997-	260
ES622	Abraham Lincoln	12000	1992-1995	450
ES633	George Washington	12000	1992-1994	450
ES644	Teddy Roosevelt	10000	1993-1997	325
ES866	Thomas Jefferson	7500	1996-1997	325
ES635	Ben Franklin	12000	1993-1996	325
ES893	Noah and His Ark	10000	1996-	260
ES894	Moses	10000	1997-	260
ES1810	Joseph	7500	1998-	260
ES896	Ebenezer Scrooge	7500	1997-	260
ES1820	Bob Cratchit & Tiny Tim	7500	1998-	260
ES1823	King Henry VIII	7500	1998-	260
ES722	Musketeer Aramis	7500	1996-	125
ES1821	Musketeer Athos	7500	1998-	125
ES335	Mini Merlin	15000	1996-97	55
ES337	Mini King Arthur	15000	1997	55
ES344	Mini Sir Lancelot	10000	1998-	55
ES336	Mini Robin Hood	10000	1996-	55
ES339	Mini Noah	10000	1997	55

"What light through yonder window breaks?"

The Plays of Shakespeare

◊◊◊ Romeo and Juliet ◊◊◊

Mrs Cratchit

ES342	Mini Scrooge	10000	1998-	55
ES338	Mini St. Nicholas	15000		55
ES343	Mini Grandfather Frost		1998-	55

Collector's Club Pieces

ES900	King Wenceslaus	3500	1995-1997	400
ES856	Marek	3000	1997-1998	300
ES1824	Royal Cook NA		1998-	225

House of Tyrol

King Ludwig (from Tyrol)	3000	1989	1200

Taron & Sons

S633	Herr Drosselmeyer	6000	1992-1992	2400-3000
S322	Mouseking	12000	1993-1994	800-1200
S861	Nutcracker Prince	10000	1994-	230
S860	Clara	10000	1995-	230
S859	Sugar Plum Fairy	10000	1996	240
S854	Toy Soldier	10000	1998-	230
S881	Wiseman Caspar	10000	1994-	230
S882	Wiseman Melchior	10000	1995-	230
S883	Wiseman Balthasar	10000	1996-	230
S857	Humpty Dumpty	10000	1997-	210
S858	Mad Hatter	10000	1997-	230
S851	White Rabbit	10000	1998-	230
S1840	King Cole	10000	1998-	220
S322	Mini Herr Drosselmeyer	10000	1995-1996	100-150
S323	Mini Mouseking	25000	1996-	55
S324	Mini Prince	25000	1996-	55
S346	Mini Clara	25000	1998-	55
S329	Mini Kriss Kringle	20000	1996-	55
S328	Mini Herr Schneemann	20000	1996-	55
S330	Mini King Ludwig	10000	1995-	55
S340	Mini Three Wisemen	10000	1997-	150

Ulbricht

000119	Herr Drosselmeyer	5000	1996	228
000120	Mouse King	5000	1996	228
000121	Clara	5000	1996	219
000122	Prince	5000	1996	219
000165	Toy Soldier	5000	1998	238
000129	Thomas Edison	1500	1996	270
000146	Henry Ford	1500	1997	260
000148	Alexander Graham Bell	1500	1998	250
000136	Juliet	5000	1997	230
000142	Shakespeare	5000	1997	236
000156	Romeo	5000	1998	236

000141	Tin Woodsman	5000	1997	230
000150	Dorothy	5000	1998	230
000151	Cowardly Lion	5000	1998	240
000123	Scrooge	5000	1996	228
000145	Bob Cratchit	5000	1997	236
000149	Mrs. Cratchit	5000	1998	230
000144	Eagle Dancer	3000	1997	240
000157	White Buffalo	3000	1998	210
000253	Bill the Biker		1996	198

Ulbricht (Distributed by Midwest, retired 1996)

09584-3	Scrooge	2500		200
09577-5	Bob Cratchit	2500		210

12041-5	Ghost Present	1500		170
17021-2	Ghost Yet to Come	1500	1996	190
18299-4	Ghost Past	1500	1996	200
07094-9	Father Christmas	2500	Sold Out	350
09531-7	Toy Maker Santa	2500	1994	210
02961-6	Victorian Santa	2500	1995	210
12665-2	King of Christmas	2500	1996	210
12960-9	Davy Crockett	1500		160
17019-9	Wyatt Earp	1000	1996	200
17018-2	Sacajawea	1000		160
12959-3	Johnny Appleseed	1500	160	
12800-8	Paul Bunyan	1500	170	
03656-3	Herr Drosselmeyer			160
03666-2	Toy Soldier			154
03665-5	Prince			154
04510-7	Mouse King			160
03657-0	Clara			124
00-0109	Teddybear Maker	500	1996, Sold Out	450
32-450	Woodpecker (Event)		1997, Sold Out	50
000000	Penguin (Event)		1998	50

Merck
Old World Christmas

7210	Alpine Woodland Santa		165
7212	Victorian Father Christmas		165
7214	Jolly Old Elf		145
7215	Weihnachtsmann		199
7238	Candy Cane Drummer		95
72550	Honor Guard		145
727	Dortmond Drummer		145
7274	Fussen Father Christmas		165
7276	Wildkirchen Father Christmas		165
7278	Giessener Gardener Father Christmas		145
7283	Wyker Viking		145
7285	Olbenhau Toy Maker		165
7295	Schleswig Sandman		145
7295	Snowman		145
7219	Santa & Reindeer,	1000	199
7222	Black Forest Santa		145

Architecture Rekindles the Warm Glow of Christmas

By Matthew Rothman

For more than a decade it has become a popular tradition for individuals and families to collect Christmas-themed architecture. Many of these pieces are lighted and make brilliant displays to share with friends and relatives when they gather to celebrate the holiday festivities. Let us take a moment and explore the world of Christmas presented by many of today's more popular collectible manufacturers.

DEPARTMENT 56

Department 56 of Eden Prairie, Minn., introduced the world to six lighted buildings in 1976. This was the beginning of a collectible series titled the Original Snow Village. The name Department 56 originated by an identifying system used by Bachman's, a retail floral company. The department for the wholesale gift imports division was No. 56. The company's success in collectibles led it to incorporating in 1984 and retaining this unique name.

The Department 56 company offers the collector several series of villages. Many of these have ties to the Christmas theme. Of the villages, best known for its holiday cheer is the Christmas in the City Series, which

portrays the hustle and bustle of shoppers dashing about trying to complete their Christmas shopping. You can almost smell the chestnuts roasting by street vendors as you admire the city streets dressed up in all the pageantry of the holiday season. It's a window shopper's delight.

This series began in 1987 and consists of 44 lighted pieces. Fifteen lighted buildings are current and 29 pieces have been retired, including two numbered limited editions.

Another series has the enchantment coupled with the imagination of childrens' dreams of Santa Claus and his elves. The North Pole Series made its debut in 1990, with Santa's Workshop as the first introduction. This series includes 35 lighted buildings. Eighteen buildings are currently available and 17 are retired.

In 1998, limited to a Year of Production piece, came the introduction named Elsie's Gingerbread Shop. It's a place of retreat for those busy elves during the exhausting holiday season to relax and drink a hot cup of cocoa as they munch on Mrs. Claus' original gingerbread cookies. This piece includes a smoking chimney with an essence of cinnamon that enhances any Christmas collector's display.

LEFTON COLONIAL VILLAGE

George Z. Lefton Co. of Chicago was founded in 1941 and was originally a ceramics and porcelain business until, in 1987, it entered the popular Christmas collectibles market with the introduction of the Colonial Village Collection. The village represents a simpler time, a place where quaint shops, charming inns and places of worship were a common sight. Each building comes with a deed of title and a biography that gives meaning to the collection.

There are more than 127 buildings in the Colonial Village Collection. Ninety of these architectural structures have some connection with the Christmas season. It might be from a

wreath at the front entrance of a residence full of warmth, or garlands draped with red ribbons. Snow covered roofs reveal for the collector a brisk, picturesque winter's day in December. Anticipating the Christmas rush, Lefton Colonial Village included in 1991 such seasonal necessities as the Toy Maker's Shop and the Sweet Shop.

The list of retired buildings has grown to more than 40, and several of those are solid performers on the secondary market. Popular 1987 editions such as Charity Chapel, Penny House, Ritter House and the General Store have values of $300 or more, well up from their issue price of $35. Among more recent retirees, the Ritz Hotel, closed out in 1997, heads the list, going for about $200 on the secondary market.

While Lefton retired seven buildings in 1998, the company added eight new ones. New buildings with a Christmas theme include Grand Opera House, Wright's Emporium, the Member's Only Berkley House, and Trinity Church, the eighth limited edition (5,500).

No town is complete without people, and Lefton has responded with more than 40 citizens, with accessories, who live and work in Colonial Village.

More than 10 new ceramic citizens moved into the village in 1998, and they have names such as Captain Harrison and Jasper Cook and his daughter, Jennifer.

To add to the charm of the village, Lefton introduced in 1998 "Jennifer's Journey," a storybook tale that takes you through the community of Colonial Village. It's about a little girl's concern that her father is not spending enough time with her, when

indeed he is building a special sled for her Christmas. This series has been received well, and one of the many reasons is the imaginable world of Colonial Village.

ENESCO

Enesco Corporation of Itasca, Ill., the maker of Cherished Teddies and Precious Moments, is one of the most respected names in the giftware industry. Many of the company's lines feature limited-edition series for the Christmas season. David Winter Cottages, rich in English heritage, take his collectors through a Christmas tour: from Christmas in Scotland and Hogmanay to Scrooge's Family Home.

Lilliput Lane is best known for depicting architecture that blankets the English countryside. The sculptors have brought the flavor of the holiday season closer to the collector with pieces that glow with warmth such as Christmas Party, a Victorian house from a small hillside village in Derbyshire, England. Other representa-tions are St. Stephen's Church and Frosty Morning.

Ray Day keeps us current with Christmas by bringing Americana to the collecting world. Christmas collectors are not let down with names like Home for the Holidays and To Grandmother's House we Go.

FORMA VITRUM

Bill Jobs, the artist behind the stained glass buildings from Forma Vitrum of Cornelius, N.C., surely ful-

fills collectors' appreciating eye with Christmas specials as colorful and joyous as the holiday season. The names are as colorful as their appearances, such as Confectioner's Cottage, Lollipop Shoppe, and Peppermint Place. Offerings for 1998 include the innovation of Forma Vitrum's stained glass editions having the ability to play music. One piece, HollyDay Home, plays "Deck the Halls" and another edition, HollyDay Chapel, delivers the sounds of "Oh Holy Night."

HARBOUR LIGHTS

Harbour Lights, the exceptionally successful manufacturer of historically accurate lighthouses, has not disappointed the nautical collector. Harbour Lights has remembered the men, women and children who have represented this nation during the holiday seasons past. The first in their Christmas series — 1995 Big Bay, Michigan, limited to 5,000 pieces — is an exquisite snow-covered sentinel. Clearly noticeable is a friendly snowman standing in the front yard, welcoming guests as they arrive. Look closely and you will see tiny footprints of children left in the snow. This piece surely evokes the spirit of the

season. 1998 Old Field New York is another Harbour Lights Christmas representation.

SECONDARY MARKET APPEAL

Many of the Christmas theme collectibles produced by the manufac- turers mentioned have an extraordinary appeal on the secondary market, especially Department 56 and Lefton. The motivating factor for this phenomena is that these collectibles are either limited to a seasonal production or limited edition by number.

Collectors of real estate are always looking for that sought-after structure to finish their collection, sometimes paying three to four times the original cost of a piece, just to complete a village scene or keep in sequence a particular holiday display.

Added value aside, Christmas-themed architectural collectibles bring to life delightful Christmas feelings, and that special magic and joy has warmed the hearts of collectors, no matter what age, throughout the world.

Architecture: Price Guide

Values were full retail selling prices at the time of publica-

tion, but it should be noted that lower prices can be found

through extensive shopping.

ARCHITECTURE PRICE GUIDE

Here are the more popular pieces at retail and/or on the secondary market.
Values are full selling prices, both retail and secondary market, at time
of publication.

Dept. 56
Christmas in the City

Name, No.	Released	Retail	Value
Brighton School	1995	52	52-65
Cathedral, St. Marks 5549-2	1992	120	1400-2000
Dorothy's Dress Shop 59749	1989	70	225-375
Hank's Market 59749	1989	40	65-120
Christmas in the City 6512-9, set/3	1987	112	500-560
Bakery 6512-9	1987	37.50	70-110
Tower Restaurant 6512-9	1987	37.50	155-290
Toy Shop and Pet Store 6512-9	1987	37.50	175-250
Palace Theatre 5963	1987	45	750-1025
Sutton Place Brownstones 5961-7	1987	80	675-895
Variety Store 5972-2	1988	45	120-200
The Doctor's Office 5544-1	1991	60	60-75
Arts Academy 5543-3	1991	45	55-130
5607 Park Ave. T'house 5977-3	1989	48	60-125
Ritz Hotel 5973-0	1989	55	65-85

North Pole Series

Name, No.	Released	Retail	Value
North Pole Shops 5621-9, set/2	1991	75	85-132
Orly's Bells & Harness Supply	1991	37.50	35-75
Rimpy's Bakery	1991	37.50	45-80
Santa's Workshop 5600-6	1990	72	285-525
Tin Soldier Shop 5638-3	1995	42	42-70
Popcorn & Cranberry House 56388	1996	45	60-90
Elfie's Sleds & Skates 5625-1	1992	48	48-73
Beard Barber Shop 5634-0	1994	27.50	27-36
The Glacier Gazette 56394	1997	48.00	48-50
North Pole Post Office 5623-5	1992	45	55-58
Santa's Bell Repair 56389	1996	45	45-48
Express Depot 5627-8	1993	48	48-50

Lefton Colonial Village

Name, No.	Released	Retail	Value
Green's Grocer 00725	1993	50	50-60
The Nelson House 05891	1989	35	420-450
Penny House 05893	1987	35	275-450
Ritter House 05894	1987	35	300-375
Charity Chapel 05895	1987	35	325-400
Faith Church 06333	1988	40	175-275
Trader Tom's Gen'l Store 06336	1988	40	45-50
Ritz Hotel 06431	1988	40	175-215
Franklin College 10393	1996	50	50
Grand Opera House	11260	1998	50
Hillside Church 11991	1990	60	400-450
Lakehurst House 11992	1992	55	200-350

David Winter (Enesco)

Name	Released	Retail	Value
Christmas in Scotland & Hogmanay	1988	100	190-290
A Christmas Carol	1989	135	135-250
Scrooge's School	1992	160	160-260
Scrooge's Family Home	1994	175	175
Tiny Tim	1996	150	150-250

Lilliput Lane Ltd. (Enesco)

Name	Released	Retail	Value
Chestnut Cottage	1992	46.50	35-50
Cranberry Cottage	1992	46.50	35-50
Gingerbread Shop	1993	50	50
Old Vicarage at Christmas	1993	180	180-300
Eamont Lodge	1993	185	200-300

Snowdon Lodge	1994	175	175
St. Stephen's Church	1996	100	100-150
Christmas Party	1997	150	150
Frosty Morning	1998	150	150

Ray Day (Enesco)

Name	Released	Retail	Value
Christmas in America	1996	495	495
Let Heaven, Nature Sing	1997	158	158
To G'mother's House	1997	158	158

Forma Vitrum

Name	Released	Retail	Value
Confectioner's Cottage	1995	100	125-185
Lollipop Shoppe	1996	110	110-195
Peppermint Place	1997	100	100-195

Harbour Lights

Name	Released	Retail	Value
Christmas '95 Big Bay Point, Mich.	1995	75	150-250
Christmas '96 Colchester, Vt.	1996	75	75-150
Christmas '97 White Shoal, Mich.	1997	80	80-150

Old World Christmas Collectors Club™

The
GLORY
of a Traditional Christm
The
REFLECTION
of Treasured Memories

The
Crinkle Claus®
COLLECTORS CLUB

Join our NEW and exciting Santa collector's club!

Take a peek inside and see what we have in-store for you!

POSSIBLE DREAMS®

JOIN THE CLUB

By Susan K. Elliott

Celebrating Christmas takes many forms, as collectors who belong to the following clubs can demonstrate with their collections. Classic nativity designs make The Fontanini Collectors' Club the most spiritually focused group for Christmas collectors while more than a dozen other clubs deliver Christmas themes in the form of Santas, angels, nutcrackers, Coca-Cola Christmas art and ornaments for every desire.

To join a collectors' club, visit your favorite retailer, or contact the company directly. Some clubs also provide on-line memberships via the Internet, such as Hallmark at www.hallmark.com. In most cases, members must redeem exclusive items through a retailer of their choice, or may find instant redemption kits for some clubs available from retailers to start a membership immediately. Clubs also make great gifts to help someone else begin collecting.

Some on-line club sites provide members passwords to access product information, newsletters, chat rooms and trading posts to buy, sell and trade.

Each club is different, but the best ones give members a gift for joining that is equal to or greater than the cost of membership, with a variety of additional benefits ranging from entertaining publications, binders, pins, catalogs, membership cards and offers for members-only items.

Some clubs provide secondary market information for members, perhaps a forum for classified ads, or research assistance to identify pieces and provide history. Many clubs host their own conventions or gatherings annually or biannually, tours and cruises, and some groups include local chapters. (If there's not one in your area, you may be able to start a chapter.)

More than anything else, club membership provides a connection with others who share your collecting interest. Check out the following clubs first to develop a first-class Christmas collection:

Carlton Cards Heirloom Collection Collector's Club

888-222-7898

Features: Ornaments in resin and other materials.

Benefits: Welcome kit includes three ornaments, pin, Heirloom Collector's Guide, and tote bag. Members also receive a subscription to The Collector's Chronicle and special offers.

Annual dues: $20.

Cavanagh's Coca-Cola Christmas Collectors Society

800-895-8100

Features: Ornaments and figurines with Coca-Cola themes.

Benefits: Members-only ornament, four newsletters, member's certificate and card, and special offers.

Annual dues: $25.

Membership size: 15,000.

Issues for members: One per year.

Christian Ulbricht Collectors' Club

800-770-2362, www.culbricht.com

Features: German-produced nutcrackers and other wooden designs.

Benefits: Newsletter, catalog, invitations to special events, gift, exclusive offers.

Annual dues: $45.

Charter year: 1998.

Christopher Radko Starlight Family of Collectors, Ltd.

800-71-RADKO

Features: Hand-painted, blown-glass ornaments in a wide variety of styles.

Benefits: Members-only ornament, catalog, Starlight Quarterly magazine, folio for storing magazines and catalogs, pin, membership card, and ornament button.

Annual dues: $50 (new), $37.50 renewal.

Issues for members: One per year.

Duncan Royale Collectors Club

(800) 366-4646

Features: Santas of every period.

Benefits: An exclusive yearly membership bell and cloisonne lapel pin received upon membership or membership renewal. Members also will receive a membership card, certificate and catalog of all Duncan Royale Limited Editions. There is a newsletter and exclusive members-only figurines available.

Annual dues: $30.

Enesco Treasury of Ornaments Collectors' Club

630-875-5404, www.enescoclubs.com

Features: Resin ornaments.

Benefits: Membership gift, members-only pieces, publication, membership card, catalog.

Annual dues: $22.50.

Fontanini Collectors' Club

800-729-7662, X394

Features: Italian-designed nativities in resin.

Benefits: Exclusive club gift, members-only editions, newsletter, advance notification of introductions and retirements, binder, special invitations to Fontanini Personal Tour events, membership card, symbol of membership pin.

Annual dues: $22.

Issues for members: Club Symbol of Membership Gift and members-only Nativity Preview Edition.

Hand & Hammer Collector Club

800-SILVERY

Features: Sterling silver ornaments.

Benefits: Updated list of ornaments and catalog.

Annual dues: none.

Old World Christmas Collectors' Club

800-965-7669, X160

Features: Hand-painted, blown-glass ornaments and wooden nutcrackers.

Benefits: Membership gift, members-only piece, membership card and buy-sell service, video, collectors' guide, Old World Christmas Star newsletter, and local retailer list.

Annual dues: $30.

Possible Dreams Santa Claus Network

508-543-6667

Features: Santas in Fabriche.

Benefits: Exclusive club gift, members-only piece, membershp card and buy-sell service.

Annual dues: $25.

Hallmark Keepsake Ornament Collector Club

800-523-5839 and Gold Crown Stores

Features: Ornaments in a wide variety of materials and subjects.

Benefits: Early mailing of Dream Book and events, exclusive club ornament, members-only piece, membership cards, local chapters and special

MORE CHRISTMAS AND OTHER SUBJECTS

events, buy-sell service and Collector's Courier newsletter. With more than 300,000 members, this is the world's largest collector club.

Annual dues: $22.50.

Polonaise Collector's Guild

(212) 924-0900, X214

Features: Blown glass ornaments, some in boxed theme sets.

Benefits: Exclusive club gift, members-only piece, pin, video and newsletter.

Annual dues: $50.

Seraphim Classics Collectors Club

800-729-7662

Features: Angel figurines, ornaments and plates in resin.

Benefits: Quarterly publication, catalog, pin, exclusive club gift, members-only piece and membership card.

Annual dues: $55.

Steinbach Collector's Club

212-924-0900, X281

Features: Nutcrackers made in Germany.

Benefits: Gift nutcracker, history of the Steinbach factory, brochure/newsletter, special edition club pins, membership cards, and

Annual dues: $45.

Many other clubs regularly include Christmas subjects, but cannot be considered purely Christmas clubs. Consider these clubs for their wide variety of subject matter ranging from dolls to cottages, plush to figurines, musicals to crystal.

Annalee Doll Society

800-433-6557, features poseable felt dolls, annual dues $29.95.

ANRI Collector's Society

800-730-2674, features Italian woodcarvings, annual dues $35.

Cherished Teddies Collectors Club

800-875-8540, features resin teddy bears by Priscilla Hillman, annual dues $23.

David Winter Cottages Collectors Guild

630-875-5382, features English cottage designs by David Winter, annual dues $40.

Donald Zolan Society

800-265-1020, features children painted by artist Donald Zolan.

Dreamsicles Collectors' Club

800-437-5818, features distinctive cherubs created by Krisin Haines, annual dues $27.50.

Emmett Kelly Jr. Collectors Society

800-EKJ-CLUB, features favorite clown Emmett Kelly Jr., annual dues $30.

Enesco Memories of Yesterday Collectors' Society

630-875-8540, features Mabel Lucy Attwell's cherished chubby children, annual dues $22.50.

Enesco Precious Moments Collectors Club

630-875-8540, one of the largest clubs, features the tear-drop eyed children of Sam Butcher in every possible medium, annual dues $27.50.

Loyal Order of Friends of Boyd

717-633-9898, features the variety of subjects designed by Gary Lowenthal in plush and resin bears, also dolls and figurines, annual dues $30.

Leaf and Acorn Club for Charming Tails

800-486-1065, features Dean Griff's whimsical animals from Charming Tails and other collections, annual dues $24.50.

Lefton Collectors' Service Bureau

800-628-8492, a service, not a true club, for collectors to purchase custom pins, product albums and company history, Colonial Village News newsletter, and locate Lefton dealers.

Lilliput Lane Collectors' Club

630-875-5382, features the authentic cottages of England as well as American structures, annual dues $40.

Lladro Society

888-GIVE-LLADRO, features distinctive fine porcelain scuptures, bells and ornaments in soft pastels, annual dues $45.

M.I. Hummel Club

800-666-CLUB, features the art of renowned German children's artist M.I. Hummel, annual dues $50.

Melody in Motion Collectors Society

973-882-1820, features whimsical moving musicals, annual dues $27.50.

Pocket Dragons and Friends

800-355-2582, features the endearing dragon antics of artist Real Musgrave's characters, annual dues $29.50.

Sarah's Attic Forever Friends
800-4-FRIEND, features subjects by artist Sarah Schultz, annual dues $32.50.

The 1998 Guild Year
1998 APPLICATION FORM

DAVID WINTER COTTAGES COLLECTORS' ·Guild· From ENESCO

David Winter-Artist

"Mistletoe Cottage"
1998 Symbol of Membership Cottage
Join the Guild Today!

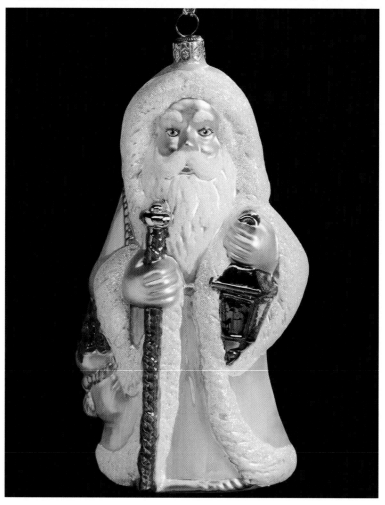

Snowbabies Friendship Club

888-SNOWBABY, features Department 56's playful children of the snow, annual dues $35.

Swarovski Collectors Society

800-426-3088, features Austrian lead crystal art in figurines and ornaments, annual dues $35.

Thomas Kinkade Collectors Society

800-544-4890, X1543, features the nostalgic subjects of artist Thomas Kinkade ("the painter of light") produced in plates, prints, canvas transfers and other mediums, annual dues $45.

Walt Disney Collectors Society

800-932-5749, features subjects inspired by the beloved art of Walt Disney films, annual dues $49.

Use this sampling of current clubs to discover the pleasures of being a member in one of today's most exciting areas of collecting. Club members have the privilege of acquiring some of the most exclusive items available for collecting. And with new clubs starting each year, the pleasure continues to increase.

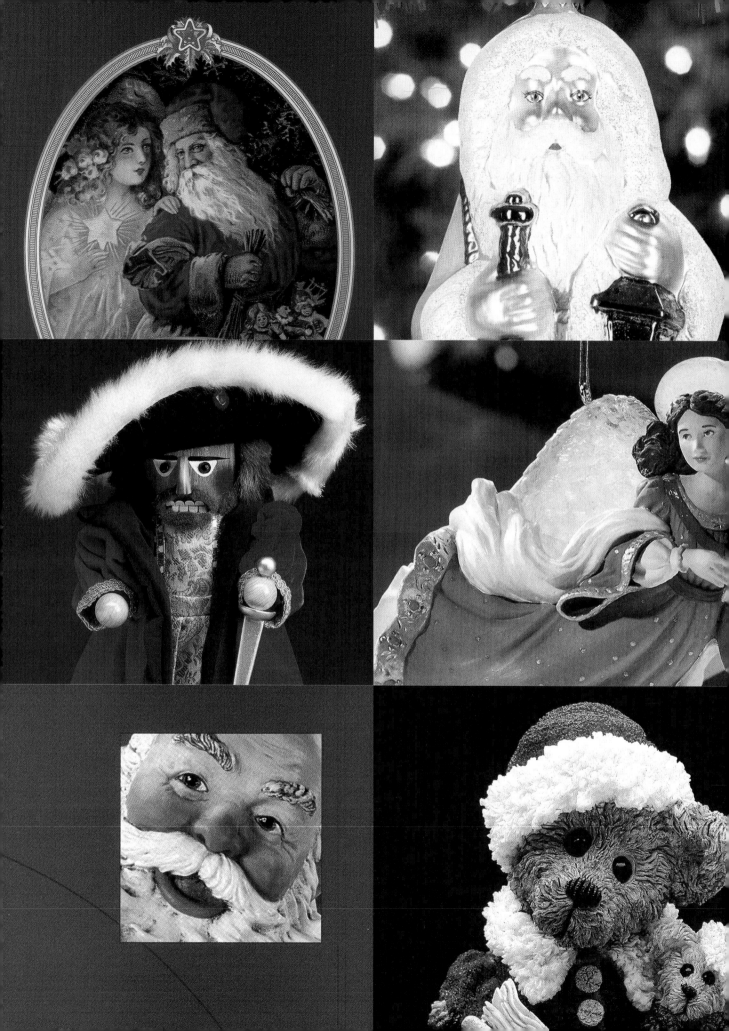

COMPANY DIRECTORY

Kurt S. Adler

1107 Broadway

New York, NY 10010

212-924-0900

Polonaise Collection, Steinbach nutcrackers and smokers

The Boyds Collection Ltd.

P.O. Box 4385

Gettysburg, PA 17325

Boyds Bears & Friends, Bearstone Collection, Folkstone

Collection, Dollstone Collection, waterglobes

Enesco Corp.

225 Windsor Dr.

Itasca, IL 60143

708-875-5300

www.enesco.com

Cherished Teddies, Precious Moments,

Lilliput Lane, David Winter

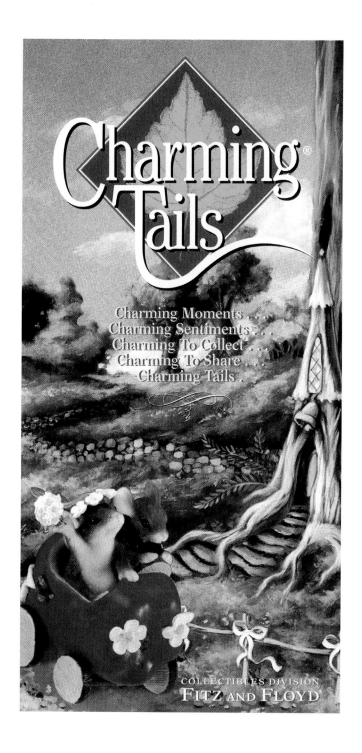

Fitz & Floyd

501 Corporate Dr.

Lewisville, TX 75057

972-918-0098

Charming Tails

Hallmark Cards, Inc.

2501 McGee Street

Kansas City, MO 64108

800-523-5839

www.hallmark.com

Keepsake ornaments

Geo. Zoltan Lefton Co.

3622 S. Morgan St.

Chicago, IL 60609

800-628-8492

www.gzlefton.com

Lefton Colonial Village, waterglobes

Old World Christmas

P.O. Box 8000

Spokane, WA 99203-0030

800-695-7669, ext. 160

Blown-glass ornaments, Merck nutcrackers

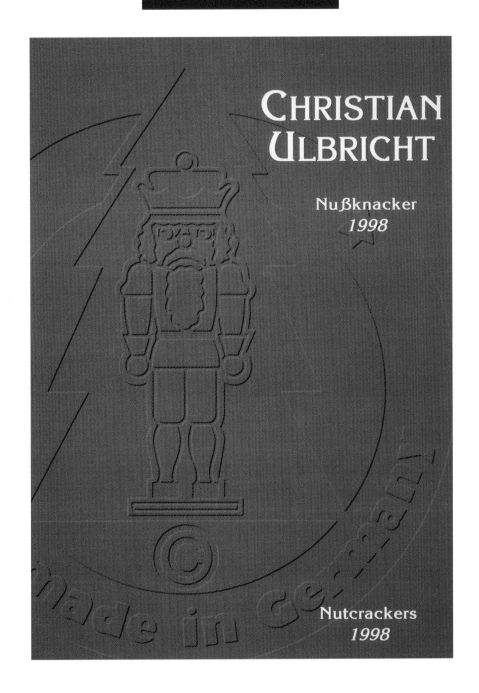

Christian Ulbricht USA

P.O. Box 99

Angwin, CA 94508

707-965-4195

www.culbricht.com

Nutcrackers

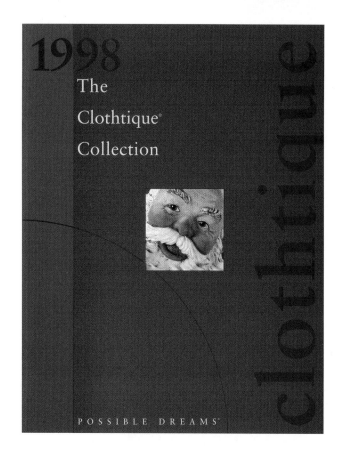

Possible Dreams

Six Perry Drive

Foxboro, MA 02035

508-543-5412

Clothtique Santas, Crinkle Claus, waterglobes

Adrian Taron & Sons Importers

801 Linden Ave.

Carpinteria, CA 93013

805-684-8615

Steinbach nutrackers, ornaments

INDEX

Hallmark Section

Blown-Glass Section

FIGURES SECTION

NUTCRACKERS SECTION

ARCHITECTURE SECTION

The Boyds Collection Ltd.

102, 111, 112, 113, 115, 116, 117, 120, 121, 140, 144, 146.

Charming Tails

107, 108, 114, 118, 124, 125, 127, 132, 133, 134, 136, 141.

Enesco (Cherished Teddies)

110, 119, 138, 139.

Possible Dreams

104, 105, 106, 109, 122, 123, 126, 128, 129, 130, 131, 135, 137, 142, 145, 147.

Steinbach (Kurt S. Adler)

153, 154, 158, 159, 166, 167, 168, 172, 178, 182 (top), 188, 189, 190.

Steinbach (Adrian Taron & Sons Importers)

148, 150, 151, 160, 173, 174, 187, 192, 193, 195.

Merck (Old World Christmas)

156, 162, 165, 169, 175, 182 (bottom), 191, 194.

Christian Ulbricht

152, 155, 157, 161, 163, 164, 170, 171, 176, 177, 180, 181, 183, 184, 185, 186.

Lefton Colonial Village

196, 198, 199, 200, 201, 202, 203, 204, 205, 206, 208, 209, 211, 212, 213, 214, 215, 216, 217, 218, 219, 220, 221, 222, 223, 224, 225, 226, 228, 229.

David Winter (Enesco)

207, 210.

· CONTRIBUTORS ·

Melanie Benham

Melanie, the author of the section on blown-glass ornaments, and her husband, Brad, launched a contemporary blown-glass ornament newsletter in 1996 called Glitter. Shortly thereafter, they unveiled their Web site, www.glitternews.com. Within months of the debut of the newsletter, they became the largest secondary market brokers for contemporary blown-glass ornaments in the United States.

The Benhams and Glitter are widely respected authorities on contemporary blown-glass ornaments and the secondary market for these collectibles. In what little spare time she has, Melanie writes articles for collectible magazines and does seminars on collecting ornaments.

Meredith J. DeGood

Meredith, who contributed the overview and prices on Hallmark ornaments, is co-owner of The Baggage Car collectibles shop in Des Moines, Iowa. Meredith and her husband publish five times a year a newsletter containing current prices for a wide range of the Hallmark products, used by collectors throughout North America for trading

and insuring their collections.

Hallmark Cards Inc. has been referring collectors to The Baggage Car for more than 13 years. Hallmark does not keep any stock for more than one year, so when a collector breaks a piece, the company provides a list of secondary market dealers to aid the collector in obtaining a replacement. Meredith is honored to be at the top of every list Hallmark has published.

Susan K. Elliott

Susan wrote the Introduction and the section on clubs, and served as an invaluable source of advice on this book. As executive director of NALED (National Association of Limited Edition Dealers), she is the author of the Complete Source Book, an indispensable source for gift and collectibles retailers.

Dean A. Genth

Dean, who contributed the section on figurines, is a national authority on the secondary markets for M.I Hummel, Precious Moments and Swarovski Silver Crystal. He owns Miller's Hallmark & Gift Gallary in three Ohio cities: Cincinnati, Eaton and Xenia.

Matthew Rothman

Matthew, our architecture contributor, writes a column on collectible real estate for Collectors Mart magazine, as well as a monthly column on Harbour Lights collectibles for the Lighthouse Digest. He owns Lighthouse Trading Company and The Exchange, a secondary market brokerage service specializing in Harbour Lights and other retired and limited collectibles.

Susan Ford Wiese

Our expert on nutcrackers, Susan owns Susan Ford & Co., a Christmas store specializing in nutcrackers, Santas and European glass. She also publishes a semiannual newsletter, Nutcracker News, and resides on the Internet at www.nutcrackersco.com.

Also, special thanks go to the companies that provided pictures and information. They are Kurt S. Adler, Boyds Collection Ltd., Enesco Corp., Fitz & Floyd, Hallmark Cards Inc., Geo. Z. Lefton Co., Old World Christmas, Possible Dreams, Christopher Radko, Adrian Taron & Sons, and Christian Ulbricht USA.